STRAIGHT TALK
FROM THE HEARTLAND

STRAIGHT TALK
FROM THE HEARTLAND

ED SCHULTZ

10 ReganBooks
Celebrating Ten Bestselling Years
An Imprint of HarperCollinsPublishers

HarperCollins books may be purchased for educational, business, or sales promotional use. For information please write: Special Markets Department, Harper-Collins Publishers Inc., 10 East 53rd Street, New York, NY 10022.

FIRST EDITION

Designed by Publications Development Company of Texas

Printed on acid-free paper

Library of Congress Cataloging-in-Publication Data has been applied for.

ISBN 0-06-078457-1

04 05 06 07 08 PDC/RRD 10 9 8 7 6 5 4 3 2 1

To my mother, Mary Schultz, whose love of education set me on a lifetime journey of learning, and to my father, George Schultz, an honorable and good man who taught me to understand and engage in the world around me. And, finally, to my wife Wendy, who opened my heart and my mind and inspires me each day to be a better man. To have someone believe in me and stand beside me the way Wendy does has truly been a blessing in my life. She is the greatest wife a man could have.

CONTENTS

Part I

THE VOICE OF LIBERTY

Who *Is* That Guy?

I have this vision.

In it, all those right-wing radio talk show hosts and industry gurus who said progressive talk radio couldn't make it are staring incredulously at the radio speaker with my voice booming out the unfiltered truth about what's *really* going on in America. Like Butch Cassidy and the Sundance Kid running for cover from a relentless posse, I hear them ask, "Who *is* that guy?"

It's me. Big Eddie. The brain, the heart, and, yes, *the mouth* behind the fastest growing syndicated radio talk show in America: *The Ed Schultz Show.* They said we wouldn't make it. They said it couldn't be done. Yeah, well, here I am.

Let me tell you about myself. You already know my name: Ed Schultz. People call me Big Ed, and from the cover photo you can see I come by my nickname honestly. I'm big: 6′2″ and 250 pounds, although one of those statistics might be fudged. I'm fifty years old, and you can see I am devastatingly handsome. The truth is, the touch-up artist was probably hospitalized with carpal-tunnel syndrome after the work she did on my mug. I'm married for the second (and final) time to Wendy Schultz. Together, we have six kids from our respective first marriages—all adults, now.

How did a prairie-dwelling, red meat-eating, gun-toting former conservative become the hope of liberal radio? It all started with this annoying habit I have of speaking my mind. Sometimes when I open my mouth all hell breaks loose. Other times I feel like a voice in the wilderness and I wonder, "Does anybody get this?"

This time, the right man was listening.

Big Eddie was coming through loud and clear.

When Wendy and I attended the State of the Union Address in January 2003, we had no idea how profoundly it would change our lives and begin to re-sculpt the landscape of American talk radio. I came to Washington, D.C., unsettled by the changes in America. The economy was floundering. We were on the eve of war. The mainstream press had largely been cowed by the administration and a climate of fear that had allowed the Patriot Act to pass almost un-challenged and unread through Congress. The neocons had hi-jacked the Republican Party and, it seemed, America itself. The Democrats looked weak and ineffective.

Right-wing talk radio was spewing its propaganda relentlessly, de-crying liberals as unpatriotic, angry, hateful, and just plain loony. And it was working. Democrats were growing frustrated with the constant hammering they were taking: Three hours of Rush Lim-baugh. Three hours of Sean Hannity. Three hours of Michael Savage. Three hours of Michael Reagan. The list goes on and on. I believe if Rush Limbaugh had been a liberal in 2000, Al Gore would be presi-dent today. That's the difference talk radio can make.

I don't view this as a grand conspiracy, despite the fact that out of more than five hundred talk show hosts in America, only about forty are liberal or progressive. Rush Limbaugh made conservatism profitable. Some say he saved the AM dial, and maybe he did. But somewhere along the line, the industry got vapor-locked into believing that progressive talk radio couldn't survive and thrive in a nation split right down the middle between Democrats and Republicans.

I'm here to prove that isn't so.

It all comes down to business and ratings. It doesn't matter what your affiliation is. The big question is: *Are people listening?* We're entertainers, not journalists. This isn't brain surgery.

It's simple. If you get ratings, you get to keep the job. Merchants line up to advertise on your show. It's incredible: We sell thin air for hard cash. And Merlin thought *he* was a magician! I'm half-kidding. There's real value in airtime. Listeners make decisions based on what they hear on talk radio. That's why this is such a dangerous time for our nation. Talk radio today is dominated by a conservative mindset that is all too often mean-spirited and intentionally dishonest. There is no balance. America *thrives* on diversity of opinion. I truly believe that's part of the reason we're not thriving now. The America I love has become an America of haves and have-nots. There's an economic greed machine at work here that is swiftly creating a two-class system. That worries me. Where's the morality? Where's the justice?

All of this dishonesty and imbalance in the media and the Bush administration was a real burr under my saddle when I arrived in Washington to watch President Bush deliver that State of the Union. I'd had enough! The day before the president's speech, I was one of forty other liberal talk show hosts taking part in a seminar sponsored by Tom Athans, founder of Democracy Radio, an organization aiming to restore objectivity to talk radio.

As part of the program, the talk show hosts were asked to speak. I had no idea at the time that this was really an audition. Tom, a former Congressional staffer and Air Force veteran, was looking for someone with the moxie to stand up against the juggernaut of right-wing radio. When I got on stage, I did what I always do—I let 'em have it. I said, "Democrats cannot combat nine hours of right-wing radio with a ten-second sound bite on the five o'clock news. It's not going to work! You are being out-worked and out-organized. Until you fight back, you're just going to keep getting beaten up!"

Afterward, Tom Athans pulled me aside. "You're my guy," he said, and then he told me about his dream to bring a progressive voice to America's airwaves. It was far from easy, but today I have a nationally syndicated show, I'm on satellite radio, I've been featured on the *Today* show, the cable shows are calling, and *Esquire* made me the Man of the Month in February 2004. (I was against it until I found out I didn't have to pose naked.) Is my head spinning? Sure. I made the leap from a regional talk show to the national stage.

Some people have tried to anoint me the savior of "liberal" radio. Look, big as my ego is, even I know that's a reach. This is a start. Like the farmers in the heartland who feed this country, we're planting the seed. And it's growing. But you know what? I am the right man for the job. It sounds boastful, but it's a matter of confidence. I believe in myself. I am secure in my philosophy. Dizzy Dean said, "It ain't braggin' if yuh kin do it." I think I can. I *know* I can.

The righties know it, too. Otherwise, why would the attacks be so virulent from Hannity and the gang? Even Limbaugh has started taking shots at me, calling me that "poor little guy" from North Dakota. Yeah, well, everybody has an opinion. Everyone I know has an opinion about *me*. I'm brash, egotistical, aggressive, passionate, big-hearted, talented, pugnacious, and meaner than a snake—those are some of the opinions. Like opinions on almost everything in America today, the ones about me are extreme.

So which one of those descriptions really applies to me? The truth is, probably all of them. I don't toe any party line: I take my stands based on judgment, compassion, and good old horse sense, no matter what I'm *told* I should believe. And today that really throws some people off. It's ironic. Here I am, an average American, more blue collar than white, but I'm not *allowed* to be in the middle. In today's America—especially on the political landscape—you're supposed to be either right or left. Conservative or Liberal. We all get labeled and boxed, and you know what? That's just plain dishonest. It doesn't do me justice. It doesn't do *you* justice. We're more complicated than that. America is more than black and white. It is brown and yellow and red, white, and blue. *That's* the honest truth.

Honesty. It's a rare commodity in the media today. We hear half-truths. Omissions of the truth. We are intentionally misled. The truth may be right before our eyes, but some right-leaning talking head tells us it isn't so, and too many people believe it. I can't remember a time when I had so little trust in what my leaders were telling me. Thank God for a free press, and yet even the media has fallen short. We don't verify or challenge official sources nearly enough. If it looks like bullshit and smells like bullshit, it probably is bullshit. As an industry, we're soft. And even when a journalist does ask questions—simply asks questions—he is vilified as anti-American. Good journalism is almost against the law nowadays. When did seeking the truth become anti-American?

My point is that I always strive for honesty. My parents instilled it so deeply in me, I just don't *feel good* if I don't say what's on my mind—even if it's unpopular. Now that I'm writing my first book, I am intensely aware of how liberating and painful this project might be. Talking about the glory days is easy. Revealing the warts, examining the contradictions, and exposing past bad behavior? It will hurt. But it will make for some good reading.

I'll tell it like it is.

The prospect of writing this book truly humbled me. (Admittedly, the word humble has rarely appeared in the same sentence with the name Ed Schultz, but in this case I'll make an exception.) After some people in New York publishing circles contacted me about writing a book, I protested, "I think if you write a book, you ought to have *done* something!" But my friends and my wife Wendy kept ticking off the list of things I've done and the places I've been, and it started to sink in that maybe I do have something to say. The more I thought about it, the more I realized that I *do* have a story to tell.

It's more than the story of one man telling it like it is from a windy North Dakota prairie; it's about what I've seen. It's about the people I touch and those who touch me. Like the listener who e-mailed me to say, "I had to decide between buying milk or gas today." Man, that hits home. These are my people, my listeners. I take my show on the road to Washington, D.C., and to the struggling rural communities that dot the landscape of the heartland. I make that effort every day because I've seen the poverty. I've seen the way the middle class in America is being gutted by a government that is increasingly by the rich and for the rich. My listener is the working stiff. Joe Six Pack. The mother who scrounges loose change because, when gas rises above $2 and milk is over four, she's in a pinch. Life on Wall Street is great, but it's life on Main Street that people are concerned about. My people have grease on their hands, sweat on their backs, and damn little to show for it.

Hell yes, I have a story to tell.

"You know why it never dawned on you to tell your story?" a friend said. "Because you're so busy looking ahead, you never bother looking behind you." Bingo. That's me. That's why I like the term *progressive.* It's positive—optimistic—and that's how I see myself. I have faith in America. I have faith in Americans. I know we're smart enough to handle the truth. Once we understand the problem, we can fix it.

So I decided to write the book. I mean, how hard could it be? Limbaugh did it. Hannity did it, and he even got most of the punctuation right. Though this book offers my own brand of good old-fashioned straight talk from the heartland, it would be short a few lines of common sense if not for Wendy. She and I met and married six years ago, the second marriage for each of us, and it is no exaggeration to say she changed—no, *transformed*—my outlook on life. She's my most trusted advisor, my best friend.

It all started with a baloney sandwich.

My first date with Wendy was at the Salvation Army cafeteria in Fargo, North Dakota, where I live and work. She was this classically beautiful, blue-eyed blonde, who managed a homeless shelter. I was a hard-charging, what's-in-it-for-me conservative radio talk show host. That's right. I said *conservative*. Republican. A shade right of Atilla the Hun.

So there we were, Beauty and the Beast, dining on baloney sandwiches with the homeless. There were Vietnam War veterans, Gulf War veterans, and other hard-luck cases all around me: The King of Fargo Radio, in creased slacks and a crisp shirt, fresh from signing a big-money, ten-year contract with Clear Channel Radio. I was pretty full of myself when I walked through those doors that day.

I left feeling pretty small, and I'll tell you why. More than once on the air I'd lambasted the homeless as lazy and the unemployed as freeloaders. In that moment, guilt swamped me. I got a lump in my throat, and it wasn't the baloney. Then some of the guys recognized me.

"Hey, you're Big Eddie!"

"You're the man, Ed!"

Their adulation embarrassed me further. I didn't see it then, but that Big Eddie was fading away. A baloney sandwich, a lovely blonde with wise eyes, and a group of straggly-haired homeless men: This reality check changed everything.

Those faces haunted me. I remember thinking to myself, "You know, maybe you're not the most important thing in the universe." I haven't looked at the world in quite the same way since.

To this day, certain people question the sincerity of my move from "conservative" to "liberal." They suspect that this was a career move. Huh. Some career move. In a medium dominated by hard-right talkers, what I was doing looked a lot like career suicide. But it was simply a change of heart. A recognition that the world had a few more shadows than I had noticed before. How could I not talk about that? I had to be true to myself. I had to be true to my listeners.

Now before we go any further down this path toward sainthood, let me assure you—I know others will—that I can still be a horse's patoot. One of my most ignominious moments came in 1988, as I was doing radio play-by-play for North Dakota State University in Fargo. The Bison were playing Northern Michigan. There was something in the air that September day. There was lots of drinking and rowdy behavior in the stands. By the fourth quarter, the crowd in front of the broadcast booth was getting ugly. Suddenly, a whiskey bottle came hurtling through the glass and struck my co-announcer, Gary Barta, in the belly. Glass rained down on us—all over me. It could have taken out my eye, and the close call enraged me.

We were live on the air, but to this day I don't know exactly what I said. Some people say I spoke in a language Dick Cheney would understand. All I know is that I threw down my headphones and waded into the crowd looking for the person who threw the bottle. I almost got in a fight. I don't *think* that I would have hurt anyone, but when someone like me does something like that, it makes news. The media lapped it up. Today, in North Dakota, it's known as "The Bottle Incident."

My bad behavior made it onto Paul Harvey, and it got me suspended. It's a day I'd like to forget. But the truth of the matter is, my actions were fairly typical for someone out here in the heartland. We settle things face to face—and nobody wants to take any crap from *anyone.*

I am not a cookie-cutter liberal. I don't walk lock-step with anyone. I've got my own drum. Ed Schultz doesn't break the stereotype. He kicks its ass and sends it home to Momma. Roll over Marconi and tell Rush Limbaugh the news: The hard right tilt of talk radio is listing back to port, one degree, one radio station, one listener at a time.

In this book, we're going to discuss the issues that matter to you.

I'll tell you about broadcasting from Washington, D.C., on September 11, 2001. It was by chance that Wendy and I were there. We were on the air, arguing for a decent Farm Bill for rural America, when plumes of black smoke rose from the Pentagon. I saw the shock, the tears, the confusion, and pandemonium. I saw children crying. I heard sirens blaring. Our world would never be the same.

I'll tell you about the day I met Army National Guard specialist Jon P. Fettig's family in Dickinson, North Dakota. Jon was the first North Dakotan lost in Iraq. I will never forget the look on his father's face as he grappled with the loss of his son. I recall how heavily this weighed on Jon Fettig's young widow. I still remember his father leaning over to me and saying in a choked voice, "We listen to you every day, Eddie." Now here I was, invited into their community to share their sorrow. I kept saying, "God bless you," because it's at such times when God needs to be brought into war—after fine young soldiers like Jon Fettig have fallen—not to justify war itself.

I'll tell you about the proud ranchers and farmers in the Midwest who feed the nation and the world with livestock and grain but, in the grip of drought and uncertain commodity prices, struggle to feed themselves.

I worry about the very soul of this nation. This is the greediest generation America has ever seen. Man, I look around and wonder when we're going to think about the next generation. What kind of world are we leaving them? The wealthy need a tax cut? Sure, break out the credit card and give our children the bill. Where's the morality the conservatives talk about? Lost in the relentless rush for profit at any cost, that's where. And the middle class is getting trampled. Unchecked greed creates inequity. The hard slant of politics to the right has this country hurtling toward oblivion in ways most Americans have yet to grasp. These are dangerous times for America.

A great country requires balance in all things. *Balance.* I'm not out to move the country to the left. I'd be thrilled if we could get back to the middle. The middle is okay. You hear that, America? You don't have to be right or left. You can agree with *both* sides on some issues. I have some views that are viewed as Republican. *Bullcrap.* They're my views. I'm not ceding them to anyone, and neither should you.

In 1998, a baloney sandwich changed my life.

This book is going to change yours.

My Journey to Here

N ow that you've heard a little about my philosophy, I ought to tell you a bit about my journey to that perspective. I've been portrayed as a man tilting at windmills. Many liberal and progressive hopes are riding on *The Ed Schultz Show*. Others think I'm on a fool's errand.

Well, I'm not tilting at windmills, but I live in region that has a lot of them. The old steel windmills, which farmers once used to pump water for thirsty livestock, are still standing here and there in rural America. And now, spectacular wind farms are popping up across the countryside, generating electricity for farms, schools, and factories. People call North Dakota the Saudi Arabia of wind. I suppose I can take some of the credit for the breeze, as I've been broadcasting from the prairie for twenty-six years. While my show went national, I stayed right here. I never bought into the idea that bigtime shows and big-time thinkers had to come from big cities.

I live in a land where the weather is extreme and the people are not. Temperatures can sink to −40°F in winter and over a 100°F in the summer. The people in North Dakota—and this is true of most of the people I've met on the Great Plains—are remarkably decent and honest. Despite the fact that our congressional delegation is comprised of three Democrats, this is a conservative state.

I grew up in Norfolk, Virginia. My father was an aeronautical engineer for the government. He was a good man, and like most fathers in those days, a traditionalist. My mother was an English teacher—the grandest lady I ever knew. I lost her a few years ago after a bout with Alzheimer's. It was an ordeal that opened my eyes to the profound inequities of the health care system in America. Both of my parents are gone now, and some days I feel like an orphan. Other times, I can feel them looking over my shoulder. When I have a bad day, when I let my frustrations get the best of me and say things I later regret, I sense my mother's disappointment. She's still making me a better person.

I grew up in a turbulent time. Vietnam was raging. There were protests in Norfolk, the biggest naval base in the world. The political unrest affected my family as it did families across America. As the youngest of five children, I heard a lot of arguments at the dinner table about the war, patriotism, and protests. I thought about joining the army. My parents never knew, but I did a lot of soul searching about it. The draft ended before it affected me. Today, as this country fights another unpopular war in Iraq, I am reminded that wars fought thousands of miles away profoundly affect us at home. With a son of my own, I worry about a draft being reinstated. I worry about my son the way my father must have worried about me.

My little league football coach Bill Bazmore died in Vietnam. My sister and I thought the world of him, and it broke both of our hearts. The last time Wendy and I were in Washington, D.C., we went to the Vietnam War Memorial and found Bill's name on the wall. In my childhood memory, Bill Bazmore was an old man, but the records say he was just twenty-one years old when his life ended in Vietnam.

As a teen, I was bused to Maury High, a black high school of 1,800 students in the slums of Norfolk. It turned out to be a great experience. Although I was a minority, I never felt like one. The friends and mentors I met at Maury High helped shape my life. For instance, when I was still a third-string quarterback, my backfield coach, Joe Thornton, posted a sign on my locker: "Hustle is the Key to Survival." I still live by these words.

By the time I was a senior in 1972, I was the starting quarterback and captain of the team. Athletics brought me together with friends like Larry Bellamy, Sam Davis, Moose Battle, Byron Brown, and my wide receiver, Donnell Leigh, who caught the passes I heaved downfield. In my mind, they weren't black or white. They were my friends and remain so today.

I was a typical boy with the typical dream of being an NFL quarterback. I played college ball for Moorhead State University in Minnesota, just across the Red River from Fargo. When I arrived as a junior in 1976, Moorhead was getting ready to play crosstown rival Concordia College, a team MSU hadn't beaten in nineteen years. Jim Adelson, a legendary sports announcer for KXJB TV who liked a good controversy, came out to the practice field before the Concordia game. When he asked MSU coach Ross Fortier who might give him a decent interview, my coach replied, "See that big redhead kid over there? That's Eddie Schultz. He likes to talk." Sure enough, it didn't take much prodding from Adelson to get me going. Right out of the chute, he brought up the nineteen-game losing streak to Concordia.

Man, I *hate* losing! I said, "I don't know what happened in those previous nineteen years, but I know *I* wasn't here. But I'm here now, and let me tell you something, we're going to win." I guaranteed it, a la Joe Willie Namath. The media exploded. Bragging of that caliber wasn't done in the modest Midwest. In fact, bragging wasn't done *at all*. You just fastened your chin strap and played ball. The papers had a field day with it, and Adelson must have run that film clip of the cocky redhead three nights straight.

As much as I'd like to tell you I played a great game, that wouldn't be the truth. But we did pull it out, 14–7. Jim Adelson never missed an opportunity to talk to me after that. He liked that I was glib and fast on my feet. He said, "You know, you have a talent for this. You ought to get into broadcasting."

But I had other plans.

I had plenty of attention from the NFL scouts after my senior season. The Green Bay Packers were especially high on me. Former Packer quarterback, Zeke Bratkowski, who backed up Bart Starr in the Packers' glory years, worked me out. He loved my strong, accurate arm. Imagine, I was at the doorstep of a dream. Me, an NFL quarterback—with the Packers, no less.

That was the year Earl Campbell went first in the draft. I knew a Division II quarterback like me—even with the passing numbers I had—wouldn't go *that* high, but the Packers led me to believe that I would be picked in the third or fourth round. They took James Lofton of Stanford with their first pick. I would be throwing to James Lofton! The Packers grabbed a defensive back named Estus Hood from Illinois State in the third round. They picked a linebacker in the fifth round. The sixth round came and went. Then the seventh . . . eighth . . . ninth . . .

I was miserable and furious. The Packers called to say they weren't drafting me. They said *no* team was going to pick me. They wanted to sign me as a free agent. What? I'd gone from a third-round pick to a nobody? Pride got in the way. I told them to get lost. Well, not in those words exactly, but I was really pissed off! To hell with those people! Besides, there were three more rounds, weren't there? I was very naive.

Round ten came and went. The Jets took Tennessee quarterback Pat Ryan in the eleventh round. Finally, the draft ended when the Cowboys took guard Lee Washburn from Montana State with the last pick. The NFL draft of 1978 was the worst experience of my life. They don't dig holes deep enough to describe how low I was.

With my dreams crashing down around me, Coach Fortier—and I love him for this—made a few calls and got me signed with the Oakland Raiders, who were just a year removed from their 1977 Super Bowl victory over the Minnesota Vikings under Coach John Madden. I had another chance. I was rubbing shoulders with the likes of Fred Biletnikoff, Cliff Branch, Willie Brown, Dave Casper, Ray Guy, Lester Hayes, Ted Hendricks, John Matuszak, Art Shell, Otis Sistrunk, Ken Stabler, Gene Upshaw, and Jack Tatum.

The glory was fleeting. I got cut by the Raiders without playing a down. I had a hard time walking away from the game. I coached the freshman football team at MSU in 1978, and Jim Adelson put me to work on sports TV. I also did some sports announcing on KQWB radio in Moorhead. Still, I wasn't ready to give up on football. I signed with the Winnipeg Blue Bombers of the Canadian Football League in the spring of 1979. It was a disaster. The ball felt funny, the game was different, and I never adjusted. Mercifully, my time there was short. That summer I signed as a free agent with the New York Jets. But, again, I was cut. By then, the cold reality had sunk in: The dream was dead.

So I threw the same work ethic I'd applied to football to sports announcing, and you know what? I got pretty good. I won a few awards and built quite a following. I realized that, while I outraged some people with my brash comments, even the ones who detested my cockiness still listened. Eventually, I brought that formula to talk radio.

For all the bombast on the airwaves, I consider myself a regular guy, shaped and scarred by my experiences. I'm a man of strong family tradition, much like my father. Imperfect certainly, flawed, selfish, and stubborn, but I do my best to support my family. Every day I tell my son, David, one of the top-rated golfers at Texas Christian University, that I love him.

I work hard. Once a grinder, always a grinder. In every job, I have tried to be the best employee in the building. Maybe that's old fashioned. Hell, I *am* old fashioned, but I've never been fired. I never was a resume chaser. Never kissed ass. Just tried to do my best. Out here, on the prairie, that makes me an average guy.

Living on the border between North Dakota and Minnesota gives me ample opportunity to enjoy nature. I love to hunt. Love to fish. And since Ted Williams died (temporarily), there is no doubt in my mind that I am the greatest fisherman in the world. Most fish are conservatives—they are cold-blooded—and my experience as a talk show host helps me devise the proper tactics out on the lakes of northern Minnesota. I've developed the world-famous Big Eddie Spinner, which is so effective, walleye actually leap into the boat, fins raised in surrender. I can't tell you the secret of the lure's phenomenal success beyond the fact that it involves yellowcake from Nigeria. It's hardly fair. I used to give the Big Eddie Spinner to listeners, but we had to stop for the sake of the fish population.

I catch conservative fish mostly on the far right side of the lake. Some days, just for fun, I put a picture of Bill Clinton on the hook. They attack. Sometimes I bait the hook with the Constitution. They attack. On occasion, I catch an extremely liberal fish. It's easy to tell them apart. They're the ones wearing the Ralph Nader buttons. I usually just give them a good talking to—*"Don't screw up the election"*—and let them go.

I eat the conservative fish for lunch.

It's not about catching my limit, though. It's the solitude and the connection to nature that revives me. When I'm in the city too long, I start to feel a little like Crocodile Dundee. You cannot live in North Dakota and be disconnected from nature. This vast plain is 70,704 square miles, most of it open prairie. The Red River Valley in the east is flat, green, and fertile. Out west, the climate grows more arid. It's the same cattle country Teddy Roosevelt loved when he ranched in the spectacular Badlands near Medora. The population per square mile is *nine* compared to America's average of eighty. Even that is misleading. Much of the state's population is in places like Fargo, Bismarck, Grand Forks, and Minot. Minot and Grand Forks have air bases.

Farms average 1,200 acres. You can travel miles of back roads without once spotting another car. In New York City, there are more than 26,000 people per square mile. I exist in both worlds. I travel extensively to the East—Washington, D.C., mostly, but my home is Fargo. You know, the one depicted in the movie. Well, we might as well tackle that one head on. Was the movie accurate?

Nah. We hardly ever use a wood chipper like that. Some of the accents were exaggerated but not altogether inaccurate. I think that's what riled some North Dakotans. We're a proud state with a proud history. But we do have an image problem. When Dave Barry's gentle ribbing about North Dakota got to be too much, the folks of Grand Forks invited the columnist for a visit—in the heart of winter—to take him ice fishing. Then, to prove they were good sports, they held a ceremony and named a sewage lift station after him.

The prairie has molded my outlook. It has allowed me room to grow. My passion for winning would have driven me to success in any environment, but would I have become "Big Eddie" in another environment? I don't know. People, like trees, need space to grow. I think that explains why I see so many big personalities in the small towns I visit in Minnesota and the Dakotas.

Several years ago, when my show went regional on stations that broadcast into seven states and three Canadian provinces, I realized I might be viewed as a "city slicker" to my listeners in more rural areas. I needed to connect. Thus, the idea for the Big Eddie Cruiser was born. I took out a loan, rounded up some sponsors, bought a thirty-eight foot RV and turned it into a rolling studio. I'm like the Charles Kuralt of the Upper Midwest. I don't view my minions from the seat of a corporate jet. I see people at ground level. Flyover country is where I live. The Big Eddie Cruiser is a *Tin Cup* sort of outfit. You know, like the Kevin Costner movie. It's not fancy, but it brings me and my listeners together.

On one trip, Wendy and I fell in love with Mott, a west river town of about a thousand people. Nestled among the buttes of western North Dakota, it is the greatest place in the world to watch a sunset. We ended up buying a small house there. We call it Headquarters West. The pheasant hunting in that area is phenomenal. The people are even better. They don't treat me as anyone special, which is perfect because I've never seen myself that way. I'm just Ed, the guy down at the end of the bar having a cool one.

The place gives me perspective.

To Slay the
Right-Wing Radio Dragon

The seconds are counting down to airtime; the nation is waiting. Big Eddie Schultz, the anointed savior of liberal talk radio, leans into the microphone, headphones on, seatbelts fastened, and . . . bleeds.

On January 5, 2004, I spoke the first words of the national *Ed Schultz Show* with blood dripping out of my nose. I had expected to be bloodied, just not this quickly.

With media requests from all over the nation to bring cameras and reporters into the new studio, I allowed just one man to enter the booth with me and Tank, my board op: Associated Press writer, friend, and rival, Dave Kolpack. The humane thing for him to do would have been to stanch the flow of blood with a tourniquet around my neck. After what I'd been through, with the intense glare of the national media spotlight and the jeers from my detractors, it felt a little like an execution. Ed Schultz, the latest in a long line of liberal sacrificial lambs.

In retrospect, it's appropriate that I was bleeding from the start. So much blood had been spilled just getting to this point. Dave Kolpack wrote, "Ed Schultz is unfazed when his nose begins dripping blood a few minutes before the Monday debut of his national radio show. He called it the 'perfect prop' to open the program. 'I'm so mean, there's blood on my sheets of paper,' smiling Schultz tells his listeners, kicking off a project that members of the Democratic Party and others have billed as an alternative to conservative talk radio. In the opening monologue, Schultz, who is an avid hunter and fisherman, told listeners: 'I'm a gun totin', red meat-eatin' liberal.'

" 'I don't have to apologize to anybody for being here,' he says. 'I mean, there's no magic to this stuff. Limbaugh has proven you don't need a Ph.D. to do this. Come on. It's radio. It's people, it's places, it's happenings, it's events.' "

There you have it, my theory in a nutshell. It's about entertainment. It's about giving the listener a fair shot at the unedited microphone. It's about bringing balance back to the airwaves.

You know the list of failed liberal talkers—Mario Cuomo, Jim Hightower, Gary Hart, and Alan Dershowitz are a few names that spring to mind. Their failures convinced the radio industry that liberal talk radio couldn't work. The industry repeated this mantra so often that they failed to go back and examine why it didn't work. It's pretty basic. Why does an actor succeed in Hollywood? First and foremost, because he's an actor!

Why does a writer succeed? Because he's a writer!

Why do radio personalities succeed? Because they're radio personalities!

To be great at anything, you have to have talent, sure, but you must also understand the craft. It comes with experience. Why does Limbaugh succeed? It's more than his message. He really is a highly trained broadcast specialist. For my part, I've spent twenty-six years in radio, fourteen in television. I'm part of a radio station team that won two Marconi Awards and a Peabody in 2002. I've also won two Eric Sevareid Awards.

Ann Coulter gets it wrong. Dismissing liberal radio, she wrote, "People don't want liberal hectoring being piped into their homes and cars. It would be like being Winston Smith in George Orwell's *1984*, forced to listen to Big Brother twenty-four hours a day. It's difficult to imagine a world in which people voluntarily choose to listen to liberals. There is no evidence that it has ever happened."

As a member of the party that can't count, Coulter fails to explain why, in a country in which more people voted for Al Gore than George Bush, those same people wouldn't be compelled to discuss so called "liberal" issues. Gee whiz, in the popular vote, Bush couldn't beat a man in some sort of coma and John Ashcroft couldn't beat a dead man in his last senatorial race. They complain about dead Democrats voting in Chicago. These guys can't even beat dead candidates!

Not to be too hard on Al Gore. Since drinking from Howard Dean's juice cup, Gore has been giving Bush hell. If he had shown that kind of fight in the election, he would have won—not lost his own state of Tennessee. But I'm glad he has discovered the fire within.

We need more honest debate in America.

When it was announced that Democracy Radio had chosen me to lead the charge against the conservative talk radio dragons, I was invited on C-SPAN, MSNBC's *Scarborough Country,* and *Buchanan & Press,* among others. Often, I was expected to out-shout two conservatives, which turned out to be about fair. After I had sliced and diced nearly everyone, including Ed Meese, the former Reagan drug czar who defended Rush Limbaugh's drug abuse, the cable shows stopped calling. Ann Coulter, who was supposed to debate me on one show, mysteriously couldn't make it.

Curious, isn't it? It's all fun and games when there's no one to fight back. The righties can dish it, but they can't take it. Why did they get so worked up about Michael Moore's *Fahrenheit 9/11*? Because they met up with a liberal who could go bare-knuckle brawling with the best of them. Why have they complained about the challenge to their conservative radio supremacy? Because the jig is up. They're feeling vulnerable. Remember how invincible Mike Tyson was until Buster Douglas mustered the courage to go toe-to-toe with the unbeatable? Tyson was exposed. The same thing is happening now. It has to happen. For the sake of this country and the First Amendment, balance must be restored to the airwaves.

There has been an unprecedented consolidation of the media. If these mega-corporations—which control television stations, radio stations, book publishers, movie studios, and magazines—are bound by a conservative company dictate, diversity in the marketplace vanishes. If ownership politicizes the media companies, as has happened with Fox News, opposing views are stifled. The result is a self-censorship every bit as effective as a government-imposed one. In effect, we're burning our own books.

Does a mega-corporation automatically restrict all programming to reflect a certain political view? No. I still believe that a corporation exists first and foremost to make money. If there's a demand for liberal entertainment, somebody will want to sell it. For instance, Fox Network is owned by News Corp. The company also owns thirty-four television stations, DirectTV, National Geographic Channel, FX, 20th Century Fox, the *New York Post,* HarperCollins Publishers, and its imprint, ReganBooks, the publisher of this book. ReganBooks has a reputation for publishing a broad spectrum of thought from Sean Hannity to Michael Moore's best-seller, *Stupid White Men.*

In my case, as a radio station operations manager and regional talk show host, I work for the biggest radio company of them all, Clear Channel, owner of 11 percent of American radio stations and recipient of 20 percent of all radio revenues. I've done my share to make them money. While I have concerns about any media company getting too big—including mine—they've never tried to edit me. Clear Channel distributes Rush Limbaugh to six hundred stations, and while I feel Rush is part of an orchestrated right-wing message, such an agenda has not affected my dealings with management. This tells me it still boils down to ratings and revenue.

When I went head to head in the time slot against Rush Limbaugh, I edged his clock in the ratings. Even Al Franken whipped Limbaugh in New York in his first Arbitron ratings. (And no, I am not connected in any way, shape, or form with Franken and Air America. We'll get to that.) We're proving that there is a demand for more than right-wing views on the radio. I am confident that Clear Channel management has recognized this. They didn't rise to number one by being slow on the draw.

What I see happening, even if there's no overt intent from the top to tilt a company one way or another, is that weak-kneed managers down the line are taking care not to offend the politics of their bosses. Also, big companies are taking fewer public relations risks. So you can end up with the Walt Disney situation. To avoid rocking the boat, Disney blocked distribution of *Fahrenheit 9/11* through the Disney-owned Miramax Films.

In 2003, North Dakota Senator Byron Dorgan led an effort to stop the Federal Communications Commission (FCC), chaired by Colin Powell's son, Michael, from further loosening media regulations that would have allowed networks to reach up to 45 percent of the nation's viewers. Fox and CBS are already above the old 35 percent limit.

The website www.TomPaine.com opined, "Just six companies own most print, radio, Internet and television media outlets. . . . Mr. Powell thinks that's too much diversity, and he's pushing the FCC to adopt rules that will allow further ownership concentration. He thinks Americans can trust a few elite CEOs to tell us what we need to know to govern ourselves." The right wing wants fewer voices because fewer voices are easier to muffle.

For help syndicating *The Ed Schultz Show*, we turned to Jones Radio Networks, one of the largest independent syndicators in the business. They've been first rate, investing a substantial amount in the show, because they believe it will fly on its own merits. There has been a lot of right-wing talk about how liberals are subsidizing this effort. Some of that's true, but what does this say about the state of the industry and its extreme right slant, when this is the only way a liberal voice can get a fair shot? Every business venture needs start-up capital, and only people who truly believe in a project will invest in it.

Democracy Radio, the funding arm of *The Ed Schultz Show*, raised $1.8 million for seed money to employ people, build a studio, and give the show two years to prove itself nationwide. This is happening because Jones Radio Vice President Amy Bolton was hungry to discover the next big thing, and she picked me. Amy, who is married to my syndicator, Paul Woodhull, is considered the diva of talk radio. She's on neither a liberal mission nor a conservative one. She's on a mission to make money.

In the beginning, there were few believers. Now there are many, but the road to this point was often brutal. No wonder I was bleeding by the time we got on the air. I'm proud of what we've accomplished. After Tom Athans and Democracy Radio chose me to lead the fight, I knew the task ahead was monumental. It was an awful time for such a venture. The economy was stumbling. Ad sales were down. We put together a two-year budget with the idea that "if we can't make it in two years, we don't deserve to be there."

On Capitol Hill, word of mouth about our plan got around. Democratic Senators Tom Daschle (SD), Kent Conrad and Byron Dorgan (both ND), Harry Reid (NV), and Deb Stabenow (MI), who is married to Tom Athans, urged me on. After I gave a fiery speech to the Democratic Caucus, Senator Hillary Clinton (NY) waved me over. "Ed, do you really think you can do this?"

I told her I thought we could.

"I'd like to help," she said. "I'll do anything to help."

"Well," I suggested selfishly, "You *could* be a guest on the show . . ."

We both laughed, but I wasn't joking. When she was on the cover of *USA Today* during her book tour for *Living History,* we called her. Two hours later, she was on the air on the regional program.

The fervor was building. I couldn't have stopped this train if I wanted to. Something about what I had said resonated with the Democrats. They believed in me. This was a calling. Wendy and I tried not to get too excited. Plenty of things could go wrong—and believe me, they did! We balanced our optimism with cold doses of reality. The naysayers were all too willing to push the reality check. When the story broke in *Roll Call* magazine, a media frenzy ensued. Somebody was going to challenge the right-wing stranglehold on talk radio! Would it be a public suicide or an execution? Hardly anyone thought we had a chance, but it was a big story.

Suddenly, I was a hot ticket on cable news channels. Wow. A Democrat with no volume control. My first cable show was with Brian Lamb on C-SPAN. My favorite caller said, "You look like a conservative. You dress like a conservative. You sound like a conservative—but the words come out different." Afterward, enthusiastic e-mails came flooding in. One said, "I saw Ed Schultz on C-SPAN this morning. Wow! He's brilliant, honest, and fearless . . . a Democrat who can save us!!"

I appeared on MSNBC's *Scarborough Country* several times until they ran out of conservatives who were willing to be pummeled. Although Joe Scarborough's politics are far right of mine, he treated me with respect. "Everybody I talk to that's heard your show says you bring something to the table that a lot of liberals don't. That's a sense of humor, great entertainment, and you've got your facts down," he told me.

Limbaugh hooted, calling me "that poor little guy from North Dakota" who would never make it. I could handle that, but I didn't appreciate him putting down North Dakota. Hannity and a myriad of right-wing parrots also took their shots.

Even the people who were kind had a look of disbelief. Ron Reagan, son of the former president, approached me at a restaurant in New Hampshire, having recognized me from television. "I admire what you're trying to do," he said. "It's very courageous." Courageous? I was just trying to do the right thing.

By this time, another liberal player had emerged—Al Franken and Air America. Naturally, Al got lots of media attention. He's a star. A brilliant comedian and a patriotic American. I didn't know if his efforts would help or hurt mine. In some respects, they hurt. We got lumped into the Air America camp by right-wing radio and cable talkers who never bothered to research it. Although we are of a similar mindset, Franken's team and mine differed in that I was a syndicated radio professional. I thought that Air America's lack of syndication was a fatal flaw in their plan, but Franken's huge name recognition ensured that they would get plenty of attention. I cheered for their success from the beginning, and I'm cheering still.

With all of the media frenzy, I knew we needed to get our show on the air as soon as possible. But the paper work was taking forever. We had three entities involved: Democracy Radio, Jones Radio, and an LLC, Big Eddie Radio Productions. We were far from ready. With a launch date of January 5, 2004, we had a little more than a month to build a studio and sign some radio stations. It was almost like D-Day. We recruited a skinny, long-haired engineer named Andre from Denver to build the studio in the Fargo radio complex where I work. We spent Christmas worrying about it. It was the darkest Christmas Wendy and I had ever spent together.

On New Year's Eve, the paperwork was finally complete. But five days from the show's launch, we had signed *zero* stations. We had not yet signed with XM and Sirius satellite radio (we are now). All we had was an Internet streaming site, which kept crashing from the overload on the servers. The studio was still in shambles.

Three days from D-Day, we finally signed two small stations, KNDK in Langdon, North Dakota, and another believer in Needles, California, KTOX. God bless them. I would start small. Very small. I could have done a conference call. I was Huck Finn with a megaphone. On January 4, the studio was still not finished. One crucial piece of equipment needed to be installed. But Andre was in Denver, snowbound with the equipment. Commercial flights in Denver were grounded. I was dying.

There wasn't time for Andre to drive a thousand miles and install the equipment. At 3 P.M. on January 4, with twenty-three hours before the much ballyhooed launch of the "liberal Rush Limbaugh," I made a call to my great friend Toby McPherson, a crop duster from Page, North Dakota, owner of Twin Towers Aviation. I told him that I was in a serious fix. He had a prior commitment: The Packers were playing the Seahawks in the playoffs, and Toby is a huge Packers fan. I would soon discover that he's an even bigger Ed fan.

Twenty minutes later, his Cessna 414 was flying toward a small airport on the outskirts of Denver where Andre was waiting. The hopes of liberal radio were riding on the wings of a crop duster from a tiny town in northeastern North Dakota, flying headlong into a blizzard. On the way back, at an altitude of about ten thousand feet in the winter sky, the heater went out on the plane. It was about −30°F. Andre was still shivering like a squirrel when he walked into the studio to save the day.

"How was the ride?" I asked.

"Pretty fuckin' cold," he said.

Toby McPherson wouldn't take a dime from me. He said it was his contribution to the show. That's the heartland for you. A spray pilot is a farmer, and a farmer will give you the shirt off his back. Meanwhile, Rush Limbaugh flies on private corporate jets. We launched a challenge to his empire using a crop duster with a broken heater.

Andre wired the last piece of equipment into place. Then, just moments before airtime, with my blood pressure soaring, I spouted blood from my nose. This was just the beginning.

I had been starring on a regional radio network that hit seven states and three Canadian provinces. Estimated listenership was one hundred thousand. I had built my show around the callers. I gave them the unedited microphone. There was give and take. The national *Ed Schultz Show* would also depend on the callers to make it a unique, democratic success. We had Hillary Clinton and Tom Daschle among the first guests, but with our anemic coverage, we just weren't getting enough calls. I knew we had listeners—not many—but I knew they were there. The thing was, liberals had been so alienated from talk radio, they didn't remember where the phone was!

And so it went, day after day. Few calls. Just me pontificating into a microphone like Rush Limbaugh, something I hoped never to do. It was excruciating. Wendy and I went to sleep some nights with tears in our eyes. I'd be lying if I said my confidence wasn't shaken. On my morning regional show, my enemies called in taunts and sometimes I lashed out over the airwaves. I confided in my friends that North Dakota, a state I loved, had turned on me.

"No, Ed," a friend said. "If that's so, how do you explain the ratings? Every enemy you've ever made is just taking the opportunity to kick you when you're down!"

A light went on in my head. I realized I had been viewing my life through a telephone line. On my regional show, the view in those days was sometimes bleak. On the national show, it was almost nonexistent. I took a beating every day. I almost came to dread the morning.

But I handled it the way Dakota cowboys do when their sons are bucked off.

"What do I do now?" asks the son, rising from the dust.

The father squints and hands the reins back to his son. "Get back on," he says.

Slowly, Jones Radio added new stations and new listeners, and the show began to grow. After two months of hell, Big Ed was back in the saddle. Within seven months, *The Ed Schultz Show* was on thirty-five stations, a far cry from Rush Limbaugh's six hundred, but still impressive growth. We did, however, land a station in Rush's back yard—Miami. How 'bout them Dolphins!

The Ed Schultz Show is proof that big dreams can start small, but all dreams worth dreaming require action. Even in these dangerous times, good things are happening in America. The voice of freedom is still alive. America is at a crossroads, and there is still time to change course. Things can change if we have the will—if we are so inspired. One day, not so long ago, a baloney sandwich on dry bread inspired me to be a better man. I have miles left to go down that path. Salvation comes in fits and starts.

A crop duster from a North Dakota town of 230 people saved the day in a deadly blizzard. My listeners inspire me each day with wisdom and good humor. My wife has helped me get back up when I've been knocked down. I've fought hard, and I've bled for this cause. But I'm only one man, doing what he can. The real question, the question upon which America's fate rests, is: What are *you* going to do?

They Call Me Angry

You have to give them credit. In their own insidious way, the people behind the right-wing propaganda machine are brilliant. They have to be. How else do you establish a 9–1 domination of the radio airwaves in a country in which more people voted for Al Gore than George Bush?

But don't worry, Big Ed has them figured out. Heck, I used to *be* one of them! (Then again, I once had chicken pox.) Diagnosis is the key. Trust me. I'm not a doctor but my wife, Wendy, is a psychiatric nurse. Don't you love that? It's great. When we sit around at night watching the talking heads on cable TV, I ask her to point out the really crazy ones. She nudges me when Cheney appears on the screen. We're still trying to get his medical records, but they're probably locked up in Rush's house.

Of course, Cheney won't even tell us what's happened in the top secret energy task force huddle. That's between him, Halliburton, and Enron. In the words of Dick Cheney, from the May 30, 2001, *Washington Post,* "Just because somebody makes a campaign contribution doesn't mean that they should be denied the opportunity to express their views to government officials." I'm glad we have somebody looking out for those poor energy companies who are scraping by on record profits.

Sure, you got a tax cut.

Now, you're paying it back at the pumps.

We elected (okay, *sort of* elected) this administration to lead our country. I just don't remember voting for Halliburton. Then, to top it off, the president trotted out crying crocodile tears, to pin the blame for high gas prices on Congress because they didn't pass the Energy Bill. Hold on there, Biff! Republicans have the majority in the House and Senate. You're in charge, and you want to blame the Democrats?

That's the kind of arrogance our leaders are getting away with.

Here's how they do it. Even when the facts don't support the position—they flood the airwaves with spin, half truths, and lies. Citizens are bombarded with so much misinformation and contradiction, they are overwhelmed. The truth is obscured. That's when you resort to Big Eddie's Rule Book: *Consider the source!* As a citizen, you must strive to be better informed. Read. Listen. Sort it out. *Consider the source.*

I've made a career out of telling like it is. Straight talk—what a novel idea. I call the shots as they are. When the conservatives get it right, *if* they ever get it right, I'll say so. If the left needs a boot in the butt, I'll give it to them. When I thought John Kerry was sleepwalking through the campaign, I said so on national radio. When he considered declining the nomination until he could legally raise more money, I said it wouldn't play in Peoria. Before Howard Dean went primal, I told him that he gave me the willies. He laughed and replied, "I'm a physician. I have a cure for that!" I must admit, that charmed me.

The Democrats owe Howard Dean. He's got guts. Emerging in a political climate that castigated as seditionists anyone with guts enough to challenge the Bush administration, Dean shot from both barrels. He gave others courage and paved the way for debate. Howard Dean gave it to us straight.

Now, if we could just get straight talk from the White House. Honesty really is the best policy, but some presidents struggle with the concept. Nixon might have survived if he had faced the American people, like Ronald Reagan finally did, and admitted his mistake. Bill Clinton didn't get it either. He got caught running from the truth. Americans don't expect perfection. We expect honesty. We're willing to forgive someone for being human. Evasiveness, half-truths, and outright lies—these are unforgivable.

This is a nation that *wants* to believe in its leaders.

The problem is, our leaders don't believe in *us*.

They don't trust us with the truth.

John F. Kennedy said in 1962, "We are not afraid to entrust the American people with unpleasant facts, foreign ideas, alien philosophies, and competitive values. For a nation that is afraid to let its people judge the truth and falsehood in an open market is afraid of its people."

Times have changed. We have an administration that hasn't come clean on the Iraq war. Our leaders have obfuscated the dire truth about the deficit and the ramifications it has for our children and the Baby Boomers whose Social Security check is in peril.

Americans love a stand-up kind of person. We respect someone who will look us in the eye and admit to being what we all are—human. President George W. Bush's inability to level with us speaks volumes about his character. Apparently, dodging accountability is *modus operandi* in the White House. We still haven't heard a squawk from him about his National Guard attendance record. Think about it. If George Bush had a good answer, wouldn't he tell us? The records that could shed light on this mystery have been "inadvertently destroyed." Isn't that convenient? I just want to know, was Nixon's secretary, Rosemary Woods, anywhere in the vicinity when it happened?

People are starved for straight talk.

I believe George W. Bush is probably *trying* to do the right thing. If he had to look regular Americans in the eye each day like I do, my bet is that he would start fighting harder for them. But I think he's disengaged, disinterested, and being led around by the nose by dangerous people like Cheney and Karl Rove. It's hard for me to believe that our president is more loyal to the average working stiff than he is to corporate CEOs. When George W. Bush supported eliminating overtime pay for Joe Six Pack, whom did that benefit? The working man or corporate America?

We are fast becoming a country of haves and have-nots. You cannot run for office in this country unless you have a lot of money. *What's wrong with that?* The American people are represented by politicians who don't win on the issues! Money controls the message. Money controls the courts. Money controls you.

I worry when George W. Bush says he's making decisions based on what he hears from God. Didn't that start with the French? Who does he think he is? George of Arc? *Time* columnist Joe Klein said it best in a piece about our president: "Faith without doubt leads to moral arrogance."

Moral arrogance leads to people flying jets into skyscrapers.

Moral arrogance leads nations into ill-advised conflicts.

Moral arrogance leads to big trouble.

Conservatives have tried to lay exclusive claim on God and patriotism. Well, let me tell you, Democrats died on Omaha Beach, too. Heroes come from both sides of the aisle. Heroes come from New York, Los Angeles, and Houston. But the GOP seems determined to convince you that God is exclusively on their side. Well, God *used to be* a conservative. In the Old Testament, he turned Al Gore into a pillar of salt. But in the New Testament, he got liberal. He started talking about caring for the poor and how tough it was to shove un-principled, rich lard asses through the eye of a needle. Look it up.

Okay, before Pat Robertson organizes a prayer chain to send lightning bolts up my ass, let's get another thing straight: I love God. I thank him every day for giving me a great life. I'm a church-going Christian. But I believe in separation of church and state. If I were president, you bet I'd pray before I sent American troops off to die, but I'd have a long chat with Colin Powell first. If my father were still alive, I'd talk it over with him, too.

But let's get back to the propaganda that disarmed the progres-sives and liberals in this country—or as I like to call them, *the voice of reason.* Guess what? We disarmed ourselves! The righties say that, because we oppose record deficits and soaring health care costs, and feel we were misled into war, Democrats are *angry.* We've heard this accusation of anger so many times that we've become self-conscious about it. *We* didn't believe it, but we feared that other people might. So we muzzled ourselves! The Bush Machine rolled right over us. They pancaked us like Wile E. Coyote under a steamroller. Holy smokes! It's brilliant. It's also mean, spiteful, and dishonest. If you simply want to engage in debate, you're branded as *angry.* If you challenge the White House disinformation squad, you *hate* George W. Bush. I don't hate George W. Bush. But I do hate what he's doing to our country.

Let me tell you something, America, even Jesus got angry. He booted those money changers right out of the temple. Now, after what Mel Gibson did to him, you know he's ticked. I am not going to give up my right to be angry. Sometimes I *do* get angry. So sue me. In fact, I'm not going to relinquish a single human emotion to the right wingers.

Rush Limbaugh heckles anyone who laments the plight of the working class poor. Forty-four million Americans are without health coverage and wish they had some medical records to hide. Limbaugh exposed his own elitism when he couldn't tell his listeners what the minimum wage is in America. For the record, Rush, it's $5.15 an hour. That's $206 a week before taxes—$10,712 a year. Rush Limbaugh spends more than that on toilet paper.

Because he is so full of shit.

I'll give Rush credit, though. Since he's come back from drug rehab, he's done less sermonizing and has actually started taking calls from people who disagree with him. (I'll bet the lines are full.) This new approach started about the time the national media began paying attention to *me*. I told them I don't screen calls. I don't have to. I know what I believe and can defend myself. I've had some knock-down, drag-out fights with callers who disagree with me. But what you'll hear me say to the caller at the end of the argument is, "Great call. Call back again."

I give the unedited microphone to Americans because I love the give and take.

Let me tell you why I have a problem with Limbaugh and Hannity. They're corporate lap dogs. I can respect a man who is passionate about what he believes. I didn't agree with Ronald Reagan on many issues, but I respected and genuinely liked him. I question Limbaugh's and Hannity's sincerity—especially Hannity. Check him out on *Hannity & Colmes* on Sly Fox News. (Colmes is the handsome one who doesn't get to talk.) Is it fair and balanced? Well, you've got drivel balanced by silence.

You can't even look Hannity in the eye! He's been slanting the news for so long, his head is tilted! It really is! Man, I'll be watching him, trying to look him in the eye, until my own head starts to tilt and—before long—my whole neck hurts. Chiropractors in America love this guy! They ought to advertise on the show. Let Colmes read the script. I want to hear what he sounds like.

These conservative talking head shows don't make an effort to get competent Democrats. They choose some shambling tomato can, give him the title of "Democratic Strategist," beat him up for five minutes, and call it balance. How does one get to be a "Democratic Strategist," anyway? Is there a mail order course I can take?

That's not real debate. The righties don't want *real* debate. I'd love to debate Limbaugh and Hannity because I don't believe they're solid on their philosophy or sincere in their beliefs. Limbaugh and the rest of the neocons don't care about you. He's got his. They've got theirs. You've got squat. But don't get angry.

Right-wing talk show hosts often sell a false premise to their listeners. They invent liberal positions. Then they attack the contrived position. How can you lose a debate when you create both arguments? It's dishonest. They claim that Democrats are unhappy when there is good news for America. Ridiculous! Democrats cheered when Saddam was captured. Democrats mourned Ronald Reagan when he died.

All Americans want America to do well. Democrats just disagree with the course America has taken. We may not agree with how we went to war in Iraq, but you can be damn sure we want to win. What is patently unfair on the airwaves today is the attempt to define Democrats as un-American.

"They *hate* America," Limbaugh says, "They *hate* George W. Bush." What kind of nonsense is that? Debate is not un-American, and it's not about hate. The ability to challenge and reform our government is what makes us *free*. Squelching debate by branding it un-American is dishonest, dangerous, and, in itself, hateful.

Dissent is our right. And, in times like this, it is our responsibility. Debate is good. It *should* cause us to examine our beliefs. If they don't hold up, change! So what do the administration and the talk show sock puppets do when they have no good argument? Attack. Vilify. Accuse those who engage in debate of aiding and comforting the enemy—which, under the Orwellian-named Patriot Act, could put you under John Ashcroft's thumbscrews. It's an old tactic. See if you can guess who said this:

> Naturally, the common people don't want war, but after all, it is the leaders of a country who determine the policy, and it is always a simple matter to drag the people along, whether it is a democracy, a fascist dictatorship or a parliament or a communist dictatorship. Voice or no voice, the people can always be brought to do the bidding of the leaders. That is easy. All you have to do is tell them they are being attacked and denounce the pacifists for lack of patriotism and exposing the country to danger. It works the same in every country.

If you guessed Karl Rove, you're wrong. No, it wasn't Ashcroft, though his pronouncements in the days following September 11 were eerily similar. It was German Reichs-Marshall Hermann Goering, circa 1939.

Rush Limbaugh was outraged the day he found out a caller (who was not allowed on the air) wanted to compare him to Hitler's propaganda minister, Joseph Goebbels. So why didn't he take the call? Because he can't handle debate. And because he is the propaganda wing of the Bush administration. Who does Limbaugh attack? Democrats. The free press. He's been doing it for years. Now, read what Goebbels had to say in 1934:

> There are no parliamentary parties in Germany any longer. How could we have overcome them had we not waged an educational campaign for years that persuaded people of their weaknesses,

harms and disadvantages? Their final elimination was only the result of what the people had already realized. Our propaganda weakened these parties. Based on that, they could be eliminated by a legal act.

The positive national discipline of the German press would never have been possible without the complete elimination of the influence of the liberal-Jewish press.

Today the open agenda is to destroy the Democratic Party. Sean Hannity's book, *Deliver Us from Evil,* is subtitled *Defeating Terrorism, Despotism, and Liberalism.* I found the book at my dentist's office.

I said, "Doc, you've betrayed me!"

"Settle down, Ed," he answered. "We just use it to sedate the patients."

But I keep thinking, what if someone actually makes it through Hannity's book? (It's the only one I've ever seen with a warning not to drive or operate heavy equipment afterward.) What if they actually equate liberalism with terrorism, or as Ann Coulter did, with treason? If you destroy liberalism, you kill the Democratic Party. And when you have one party, you get what Germany got in 1938.

"Ah-hah!" the righties are saying about now. "You *admit* the Democratic Party is liberal!" Yup, and you didn't even have to use a cattle prod, Field Marshal Von Rumsfeld. If straight talk makes me a liberal, fine and dandy. But my meat-eating, gun-toting, and revolutionary talk about fiscal responsibility throws the traditional baseline off a bit. I've even been criticized by liberals for not being "a real liberal." Terms like liberal, progressive, rightie, and neoconservative paint broad strokes, and most people run the full palette. I've been lumped into the liberal camp, but I don't believe I have to support *every* position that some party hack pounds out in a position paper.

But the word "liberal" is very positive. *Webster's Dictionary* describes "liberal" as meaning "favorable to progress or reform . . . having views advocating individual freedom of action and expression . . . pertaining to representative forms of government rather than aristocracies and monarchies . . . characterized by generosity . . . open minded."

You can look it up. You'll find it right below the word that describes hard-right talk show hosts: "libelous." If you research the word "conservative," here's what you'll find it means: "disposed to preserve existing conditions . . . to limit change."

Again, conservatives are, broadly speaking, *traditionalists.* That's okay. I embrace tradition, too. You need tradition as long as it's a *positive* connection to the past. But evolution requires a strong foothold in the tried and true past, as well as curiosity and creativity, to build a better future. It requires balance. In many ways, I'm Old School. I embrace traditional family values. I believe in morality in the bedroom *and* the boardroom. I work hard. I want my son to be as proud of me as I am of him. Because I love Dave (my son from my first marriage) and have experienced the joy of his transformation from youth to adulthood, I struggle with the ethics of abortion. But I'm not lining up to dump *Roe v. Wade,* either.

I'm a man of progress. I want things to get better for Americans— all Americans. I like the word "progressive" (which is one definition of liberal). Another good word that describes my philosophy is "populism," which "promotes the interests of the common people."

Liberal. Progressive. Populist. I won't run from any of those terms. They're positive terms. Unfortunately, the hard right has hijacked them in the same way they hijacked Ronald Reagan's funeral and bastardized the occasion by turning it into a referendum on Voodoo Economics. Fine, but at least meet the legal requirement and have the president start each Fox News broadcast with, "I'm George Bush, and I approved this message." Fox News should just end the pretense and begin running "Vote Republican" on the ticker tape at the bottom of the screen.

"Liberal" shouldn't be considered a dirty word—nor, for that matter, should "conservative." At this point, since I know labels mean different things to different people, I want to offer my personal definition of the terms I will use in this book:

Conservative	Traditionalist
Rightie	A traditionalist with a crew cut. Accessorizes with blinders.
Neoconservative	Fascist
Liberal	A direct relation to the word liberty. That says it all.
Progressive	A less strident form of liberal. Sometimes mixes with conservatives, much to the consternation of the master race, the neocons.
Leftie	More idealist than realist. Did inhale. Probably still does.
Independent	Has 20–20 vision. Sees through the BS in both parties.

Now, here are two more descriptions for you:

Democrat	American
Republican	American

We shouldn't lose sight of that.

In America today, on the right-wing radio programs and conservative cable shows, the Democratic Party is mercilessly vilified. It's more than criticism. It is an unholy alliance between the neocons and their media attack dogs.

There's a new dynamic at work here, and not all Americans have sorted through the layers. In general, the media has been there to report the news and, in some cases, defend the common man from his government. Honest reporters have provided balance. In the spotlight, governments have had to play it straighter and perform better. Circuses work in much the same way. Sometimes it is difficult to tell them apart.

But ever since Rush Limbaugh created the advocacy radio that spawned advocacy television like Fox News in the late 1980s, we lost our balance. Think about it. For the first time, an administration has the unabashed support of an entire television network to add to Rush Limbaugh's six hundred radio stations, which parrot the neocon party line. David Brock, in his book *The Republican Noise Machine,* talks about a powerful media machine that includes newspapers, networks, op-ed columnists, Christian Right broadcasting, and Internet sites with a coordinated message.

Some people will argue that the mainstream media has always been liberal and the righties are just evening the score. But I don't believe that presenting many different views on a given issue, as CBS, NBC, and ABC evening news programs still do, is liberal. Real journalism has never been about ideology. There *is* advocacy, but it belongs on editorial pages and should not be disguised as real news. In traditional media reporting, you'll find both positive and negative stories on an issue. With Limbaugh and Fox News, the mission is to tell only one side of the story. When you combine that mindset with the consolidation of media companies, you lose diversity.

Even Michael Moore couldn't get Miramax to distribute his award-winning, Bush-bashing documentary, *Fahrenheit 9/11,* because Disney, the parent company reportedly thought the film might jeopardize its tax breaks in Florida, where Jeb Bush, Dubyah's brother, is governor and lead chad counter.

Consolidation of the media consolidates the message.

Free speech is being bought up in America like real estate.

Oh, but it's still free on the street, right?

For now, perhaps, but America's children are being indoctrinated.

In February 2004, when I was on a panel with other talk show hosts at a national broadcasters' convention in Washington, D.C., moderator Mort Crim asked talker Hugh Hewitt, "How do you view your job?" Hewitt, from Salem Broadcasting, said, "My job is to defeat John Kerry."

There you have it.

My job isn't to elect John Kerry, but I do hope he wins. If he loses—and for the sake of argument say Hillary Clinton is the next candidate and fails—there are some Democrats who think it could be the end of the Democratic Party.

Here's the GOP game plan: Get the president reelected in 2004. Say or do anything. Jeb Bush is next in 2008 and 2012. By 2016, if the world hasn't ended, Neil Bush ought to be ready. If he can lay off the Asian hookers. It won't be a presidency at that point. It will be a monarchy. Your kids will be goose-stepping out to recess. Michael Moore and I will be playing checkers in the gulag with broomsticks up our asses. Your move, Mike.

That's what we're up against, America. Every fight is fixed. Stories from the righties are suspect. Let them know you're on to them. Call the talk shows. Write letters to the editor. Vote. It's liberating. As George W. Bush said, "Americans love freedom." Well, then, feel free to kick him out of the Oval Office. Even if your vote for a Democrat won't count in those new Florida electronic voting machines, it will still feel good to push that button. George W. Bush promised to unite America. Today, we are polarized. I still believe George W. Bush can unite America—by getting the hell out of the way.

Part II

THE FOUR PILLARS OF A GREAT NATION

By now, you have a fair idea of who Big Ed Schultz is. You have a sense of the hard work and commitment it's taken for my voice to be heard above the clamber of right-wing voices. But what is my message, exactly? It's a message of hope. It's a philosophy. It's also a warning.

My philosophy for a vibrant country is simple. You have to defend your country, support it economically, feed its people, and educate its youth. The Bush administration is failing on every count. I call them pillars because I want you to visualize a beautiful Roman structure. Some of you may imagine a crystalline pool beneath the roof, surrounded by beautiful women in loose-fitting togas. Hey, it's *your* vision. I'm a happily married man, and I know Wendy will be reading this. On the other hand, if you imagine seventy virgins sitting around the pool, expect John Ashcroft to kick down the door.

Or Charlie Sheen.

I choose Rome because the parallels between Rome and America are profound. This is a cautionary tale. Rome was unable to defend its borders. The Bush administration, it seems, is unable to defend ours. The Romans' diplomacy of arrogance cost the empire dearly; conquest and overextension eventually brought on Rome's own ransacking by barbarians. The only difference in our case is that we elected *our* barbarians. *Okay, the Supreme Court elected them.* It's semantics. I'll tell you what, if Antonin Scalia ever makes *me* vice president, I'll take him duck hunting, too.

Our leaders are out of touch with the struggles of middle class America.

The American worker is working harder than ever and is still struggling to make ends meet. Productivity is up. Paychecks aren't. Personal savings dropped from 1984 to 1998. One out of five American children lives beneath the poverty line. One percent of the population owns as much wealth as 95 percent of the population combined.

We're losing the balance in America. We're losing the middle class.

I'm taking about the people in America who take their shower at the *end* of the day—the guys with blue collars and calluses on their hands. The trucker who is getting his wallet drained at the gas pump. The single mother working two jobs because she is too proud to take food stamps. The elderly couple who must choose between prescription drugs and food on the table. Retired Americans who built this nation are skipping their blood-pressure medicine because they can't afford it. And when a stroke levels them, the nursing homes absorb everything, anyway. Veterans are being ignored by the very same government that demanded their sacrifice. This is the real America.

Nixon talked about a silent majority. I want to talk about a *silenced* majority. These good people have endured, and when they protest, they are branded malcontents, seditionists, and (*gasp*) liberals! They have not had a voice.

I believe when these good Americans understand the depth of the deception they have endured, when they understand how perilous a path America is on, they will take action. When they understand that the very pillars that have made America great are under siege, they will rally to protect them.

THE FIRST PILLAR: DEFENDING THE NATION

On my show, I once called the president the most dangerous man in the world and was challenged vociferously by a conservative caller. Here's why I said what I said. The man with the most potential to do great harm in the world is the president of the United States. He wields the most power and has the biggest gun; he's the most dangerous. He has the potential to make the biggest mistakes. And he's done that.

I read a story in the *Houston Chronicle* after the U.S. invasion of Iraq began in which a Vietnam War veteran named Thomas Greene said, "I thought we were above throwing the first punch." Didn't we used to be the good guys? Haven't we always viewed the moral high ground as American territory? Our case has been weakened by a shoddy, sometimes dishonest case for war. We insulted our allies. We've burned bridges. Bottom line—America's credibility with crucial allies like Germany and France won't be rebuilt until we have a new administration. We're doing all the heavy lifting in Iraq. American troops account for about 90 percent of the troops deployed! Compare Halliburton's 24,000 employees on the ground in Iraq to Great Britain's 3,000 troops.

The military is stretched to the breaking point. Veterans who haven't worn a uniform in years are being asked to leave their families, jobs, and businesses. There are plans for a draft. The Iraq War has turned global opinion against America. Even though al Qaeda has been disrupted, terrorism has *increased*. Americans are increasingly faced with disquieting images of war and the realization that sometimes we are, indeed, ugly Americans. I still believe in America as a shining beacon of freedom and hope in this world, but this administration has tarnished that image and squandered American credibility. When I saw the photographs of Iraqi prisoner abuse, I said to myself, "America is better than that. We *have* to be."

Dammit, I want my white hat back.

Meanwhile, America's borders remain undefended. What we have is a color-coded alert system designed to scare the hell out of us. What else could possibly be the point? They tell us we are going to be hit but they don't know how and they don't know when. Hmmm. Didn't *you* know that? You could head up homeland security. Check monster.com and see if there's an opening.

We have not secured our ports. We are inspecting a scant 4 percent of shipping containers. Unless bin Laden puts his return address on the shipping container—*B. Laden, Damp Cave, Afghanistan*—we're in trouble. With the dismantling of the Soviet Union, no one can account for all the nuclear material. That's disquieting. Defending our borders is the most basic military strategy. In chess, you don't attack the opponent's king until your own is secured.

The cost of the war is burdening the economy with historic debt. We're cutting key aspects of homeland defense because of budget issues. Defending America means securing our borders. The Cold War ended because the Soviet Union could not *afford* to fight it any longer. A long and bloody war in Afghanistan sapped them economically as the Iraq war threatens to do to us today.

In the following chapters, I want to talk about the dominant issues facing America—terrorism and Iraq. Like many Americans during the 9/11 crisis, I stood behind my president. I think it is the natural reaction of patriots. But I think there are lessons to be learned from such blind faith. Our American media was compromised. On one hand, there were patriots within the media who forgot that debate is always necessary. On the other hand, we had journalists cowed by events—9/11, anthrax, Afghanistan, Iraq, the Patriot Act . . . I am only one American of many who believes our leaders have made grave errors. It wasn't just the media and our government who failed us. *We failed ourselves.* It does not bode well for democracy if we do not learn from recent history. The decisions we have made will affect Americans in ways that we are only now beginning to comprehend.

THE SECOND PILLAR: A SOUND ECONOMY

First off, let's get past the "deficits don't matter" talk you hear from Dick Cheney. Deficits used to matter—back when Democrats were running them up. But now, when America is teetering on the precipice of financial ruin, suddenly debt doesn't matter?

It took the national debt two hundred years to reach $1 trillion. Supply Side Economics quadrupled the national debt to over $4 trillion in twelve years (1980–1992) under the Republicans.

Bill Clinton actually *paid down* the national debt. How did he do it? He raised taxes. It produced the longest sustained economic expansion in U.S. history. It added twenty-two million new jobs. Bush created jobs all right. Unfortunately, most of them went overseas. Only in his fourth year, after running Bill Clinton's economy into the dirt, was Bush able to tout 1.4 million new jobs. *Congratulations! Say, can you super size that for me?*

When GW took office, the government forecast estimated a $5.6 trillion *surplus* for his term. We were scheduled to pay off the debt completely by 2010! After more than three years of recession under George Bush, the national debt is $7 *trillion*. Try to imagine even a trillion. (It's a million million.) Wow. That's the number of distortions you could expect to hear on Sly Fox Network in an average day.

Unless Hannity has the day off.

Certainly, the 9/11 crisis and the cost of the war in Afghanistan are legitimate excuses for running a deficit. However, Bush exacerbated the problem with tax cuts and an unnecessary war in Iraq.

We are seeing an historic concentration of wealth among a very small percentage of Americans. This small elite includes people in government and those well-connected to the government who make self-serving policies—like the $1.6 trillion tax cut for the wealthy. If George W. Bush split the tax cut with every one of the 2.9 million persons who lost a job on his watch (the first time that's happened since Herbert Hoover), each unemployed citizen would get nearly $94,000. The top 20 percent wealthiest Americans get nearly 70 percent of the $1.6 trillion in planned tax breaks. In 2006, those who earn over $1 million a year will get a $140,000 tax cut. Middle-income people will get $566.

By then, that should cover a tank of gas.

This isn't economics. It's politics. When Treasury Secretary Paul O'Neill challenged the second round of tax cuts, Vice President Dick Cheney replied, "We won the midterms (2002 elections). This is our due." Even the president balked, "Haven't we already given money to rich people? This second tax cut's gonna do it again. Shouldn't we be giving money to the middle?"

Bush's chief political advisor, Karl Rove, replied, "Stick to principle. Stick to principle."

And what principle, I ask, would that be?

While capitalism remains the best machine to fuel a civilization, a severe imbalance in wealth is dangerous, which is why all other industrialized countries more fairly tax the rich and provide more social programs for the poor and middle class. In these largely peaceful countries, health care is a right, not a privilege. In our country, corrupt alliances between big business and government have created a stranglehold on power. This unholy alliance has left the common man unprotected.

THE THIRD PILLAR: FEEDING THE NATION

If you cannot feed a nation, you cannot *be* a nation. It becomes a mob. On the surface, in a nation that struggles with obesity, this may be a hard argument to swallow. But heck, America, you're swallowing everything else—chew on this. Dwayne Andreas, former chairman of Archer Daniels Midland, said to Reuters in 1999, "The food business is far and away the most important business in the world. Everything else is a luxury. Food is what you need to sustain life every day. Food is fuel. You can't run a tractor without fuel, and you can't run a human being without it either. *Food is the absolute beginning.*"

If global companies like ADM, Cargill, and ConAgra continue to dominate the market, they will control food the way OPEC controls oil. The American farmer is being squeezed from the land. It's happening in the heartland in the same way Wal-Mart is devouring small businesses.

These global companies are getting a stranglehold on the food industry. The meat-packing industry is controlled by four packers. Farmers and ranchers have become serfs on their own land. Bad farm policy and bad trade agreements are killing small towns, and small towns and small businesses are the heart of this nation.

Maybe you aren't convinced that food policy is "sexy" enough to warrant your interest. However, the *Third Pillar* is the single most important one. When monopolies own the food supply, they will own you politically. They will own *you*. Remember, *each* of the four pillars must be strong. If one crumbles, they all will eventually fall.

THE FOURTH PILLAR: EDUCATING AMERICA

If a nation does not educate its people, it sacrifices vision, creativity, and hope. An educated American is a productive American. This administration shorted its own program, *No Child Left Behind*, $9.4 billion. The president touts the program as one of his successes. Yeah, well, ask your local school board how things are going. Despite an increase of 58 percent to the Department of Education in Bush's first three years, schools remain woefully underfunded. That means you pick up the tab on a local level.

The crisis continues in our nation's colleges, according to a 2003 congressional study by Congressmen John Boehner (R-OH) and Buck McKeon (R-CA). The Advisory Committee on Student Financial Assistance reported that cost factors prevent *48 percent* of college-qualified high school graduates from attending a four-year institution and 22 percent from attending any college at all.

What does it mean for America if, as Boehner and McKeon say, "The manufacturing economy of the twentieth century is being transformed into a knowledge economy in which a nation's fortunes may be more directly linked to the knowledge and know-how of its workers."

The problem is that colleges don't run like a business. Until we restrain college spending, American families can't keep up. The average cost of tuition is approaching $8,000 a year. In 1982, it was less than $2,000. Even adjusting for inflation, the cost of college has nearly doubled in twenty years.

Boehner and McKeon say: "Education is the great equalizer in our nation. It can bridge social, economic, racial, and geographic divides like no other force. It can mean the difference between an open door and a dead end."

Those are Republicans saying that. If those were the quotes of a liberal in today's political climate, they would be accused of inciting class warfare.

Of course, this will work out great for the army. Given no other alternative, the poor—including many minorities—will get to "Be All You Can Be," which these days means *dead*.

My philosophy is that Americans must make education an everyday mission. You have to stay informed. If you don't do it, it will cost you. Look what happened with Iraq. Look what has happened to your economic future because of the massive—and still growing—debt. When you're dead, your children will pay the price. So I've devoted a chapter to that theme. And I'll discuss the problems—and solutions—of formal education.

THE FIRST PILLAR

DEFENDING AMERICA

THE PROBLEM

America's borders remain undefended. The Iraq War has turned global opinion against America. Terrorism is on the rise. The military is stretched dangerously thin. A draft looms. The cost of the war is burdening the economy with historic debt. We're cutting key aspects of homeland defense because of budget issues. The media and Americans themselves have failed to ask questions which has endangered American liberty.

HOW DOES THIS AFFECT ME?

If you're wealthy, probably not at all. You can always move to France. But Joe Six Pack's ass is on the line. While the wealthy and connected will find ways to avoid a future draft, as always, the children of the poor and middle class will be called to battle. And what about civil liberties? Wealth always ensures freedom. If we don't make drastic policy changes, generations of poor and middle-class Americans will pay in blood and dollars for the mistakes made in the past four years.

September 11: A Wake-Up Call to Homeland Defense

As we approached the glass walls of Senator Kent Conrad's office in the Hart Senate Building in Washington, D.C., Wendy and I saw every head staring up in horror at the television. We did not know that minutes before, at 8:45 A.M., the first tower in New York had been hit by American Airlines Flight 11 out of Boston. There were ninety-two passengers aboard the aircraft.

It would have been easy to be in denial. Just some freak accident, right?

Even then, Laurie Boeder, Senator Conrad's communications director, knew this was no accident. "This changes everything," she told me. At that moment, it seemed to me that America itself was protected by nothing more than glass walls.

I had had a vague premonition when we arrived at Dulles Airport in Washington the night before, an eerie and unsettling feeling. Wendy and I were aboard a Sun Country charter from Minneapolis with a dirt-cheap fare. (We travel the country often and have to watch our budget.) We landed around midnight. Dulles Airport was desolate. Like something out of *The Twilight Zone.* No one was there except us. There were two American Airlines planes at the airport. Our plane taxied in between them. It was deathly quiet, not a soul moving inside the terminal. The lights on the runway reflected on the two planes beside us, the only ones in sight. I can't quantify it, but it just didn't *feel* right. We even talked about it. We have always wondered if it was one of those Boeing 757s that slammed into the Pentagon a few hours later.

Fate brought us to Washington that day, just like fate decided who would live and who would be among those trapped and doomed on the upper floors of the World Trade Center north tower. In my life, I've been witness to pieces of history. Who could know this would be a monumental day in world history, an event from which other world-changing events would spring?

Nothing like that was on my mind. I was there to defend the farmers of the heartland. The current Freedom to Farm Bill was expiring, and it had been a disaster for family farms, driving them off the land. The late Senator Paul Wellstone (D-MN), a man I admired for his passionate defense of farmers, had said, "We've got the same ethnic cleansing [as in Kosovo] going on in rural America right now, and nobody cares."

Well, *I* cared. I was there to broadcast from the Capitol as Congress debated the next crucial Farm Bill for American Farmers. In North Dakota, we were in the midst of the worst drought since the days of the Dust Bowl. North Dakota Farmers Union President Robert Carlson was in Conrad's office that day. We were watching *Today* when United Airlines Flight 175 from Boston, carrying fifty-six passengers, slammed into the south tower. It was 9:03 A.M. Suddenly, the Farm Bill was forgotten.

So much of that day is a blur. When Wendy and I talk about that day and the whirlwind of events, sometimes she corrects me about the order of events. Sometimes I correct her. The world around us was moving at twice the normal speed.

Sometimes it seemed as if the world had just stopped.

I remember telling my listeners back in North Dakota what was happening as these horrible events unfolded before my eyes. I was professional, but when I listen to the recordings, I hear the anguish in my voice. Senator Conrad was calm and resolute as he spoke with my listeners, easing their fears. At one point he said, "We are a powerful nation. We can defend ourselves. We can fight back, and we will."

At 9:43 A.M., American Airlines Flight 77, originating from Dulles, where we had been just hours before, exploded into the Pentagon at 350 mph with sixty-four passengers aboard. There was a massive fireball. Even then, Defense Secretary Donald Rumsfeld, refusing to retreat, helped evacuate the victims. In spite of the pounding Rumsfeld has taken in the media—lots of it from me—I admired his courage. At 6:40 P.M., Rumsfeld held a press conference. "[The Pentagon] will be back in business tomorrow," he said.

There were lots of heroes that day, many of them dead or dying. Jackie Kruze, a North Dakota native and Rumsfeld subordinate, told the *Ashley* (ND) *Tribune,* "There was no panic, no pandemonium, no pushing. I remember one man said, 'Ma'am, be careful. Someone spilled coffee.' We saw people run toward the fire instead of away from it. Some were killed [trying]. If [victims] weren't pulled out in the first few minutes, they didn't survive."

Back at the Hart Senate Building, we were asked to evacuate. There was bedlam in the street. Panic. Fear in the eyes of the people running in the streets. I scrambled for a phone to continue the broadcast. I ended up convincing the people at a neighboring dry cleaners to let me use theirs.

It was unbelievable. Minutes before, I was just trying to kick-start my body with bad cafeteria coffee. Now, I was broadcasting reports from a dry cleaner. The script for the day was surreal. I'm sure phone lines and wireless connections were overtaxed. Several times I heard weird clicks and beeps.

Ultimately, the line went dead.

I did what every radio broadcaster does in an emergency. I ran toward trouble—the Hart Senate Building. We knew government buildings were targets and the attack was unfolding. I told Wendy, "We're going back in. I don't care what happens, but we're going back in."

I don't want to make it sound heroic. I just want you to understand the mindset of a broadcaster. When the public is evacuating, we feel duty-bound to stay behind and broadcast. In the Dakotas, as tornadoes roll toward communities, even as listeners are diving into basements with battery-powered radios, broadcasters are in the eye of the storm. It's our job.

We were back on the air shortly after 10 A.M., again with the calm Senator Conrad. He was speaking to his constituents back home, telling them what he knew, assuring them that America would rise from the ashes. I thought afterward that he's the kind of man you'd want next to you in a foxhole. He's a bookish-looking man with thick glasses that make him look like the number cruncher he is, but in spite of his even tone of voice, I saw real fire in his eyes. He loved his country. He was outraged by the attacks.

We were at war. But with whom?

While he was speaking, our eyes were glued to the television. I remember almost moaning, "Oh my God, the World Trade Center [South Tower] has just collapsed . . ."

Back home, that is what my radio listeners heard. Across the country, a thousand voices were broadcasting the same thing prefaced by,

"Oh my God . . ." As Conrad and I watched the awful scene on the television screen, we received an urgent note. We were ordered to evacuate again—this time it was official. The order came from the Capitol Police, who are in charge of security for Congress. They had learned that United Airlines Flight 93 from Newark was headed toward Washington. The FAA had halted all air traffic about a half hour earlier. Any plane in the air was a flying bomb.

We evacuated in mid-broadcast. Moments later, thanks to the heroism of a handful of Americans who had already begun to fight back, the plane would crash in a field in Pennsylvania, far short of the White House, which was believed to be the intended target. The White House had long been evacuated, and fighter jets scrambled to shoot down any more hijacked planes. We learned later that there were Secret Service agents with automatic rifles in Lafayette Park, across the street from the White House.

Outside the Hart Senate Building, I saw a man crying on the curb. Sirens howled. People flowed out of the buildings. I saw people hugging, in tears, as a thick trail of black smoke rose into the sky. It felt like the end of the world.

About that time, a portion of the Pentagon collapsed. At 10:28 A.M., in New York, the second World Trade Center tower crumbled. How can you forget the scenes of billowing dust chasing panicked Americans through the streets? Many of them looked like ghosts, covered in a fine white powder. I have a sister in New York. Like millions of Americans, I thought about her that day and hoped she was safe.

I spent the rest of the day broadcasting from my cell phone, outside of Capitol Police headquarters, the rendezvous point for the Senators and Congressmen. I was cordoned off with members of the national media. When I spotted U.S. Representative Curt Weldon (R-PA), I hustled to interview him. "This is an absolute failure of our intelligence community!" he spat. He was just rabid. Prior to the attack, Weldon had been an outspoken advocate of beefing up defense and intelligence gathering. He's now a member of the Select Committee on Homeland Security.

The crucial First Pillar—Defending America—had been breached.

Many of the Congressmen were visibly furious. They didn't know where their congressional leaders were. According to the *Washington Post,* a secret "shadow government" was already in the works. Senate Majority Leader Tom Daschle told me he was whisked away to a secret location. Most of Congress was unaware that a Cold War plan involving about a hundred "high-ranking administrators" was in place in two fortified locations on the East Coast. That's how quickly a democracy can evaporate.

The Senators were as out of the loop as Secretary of State Colin Powell is these days. As members of the media, we had been in contact with our radio stations back home. We knew what was happening in New York. As some congressmen began to leave Capitol Police Headquarters, I shouted to Senator Joe Biden (D-DE), "Senator, there are reports that thousands are dead! Do you have any comment on that?" He looked at me in astonishment. I knew then it was the first he had heard of it.

That was unsettling. You expect—*you want*—your leaders to be informed so that they can lead. Instead, it was chaos. It was obvious that there was no evacuation plan. I got an interview with Senator Richard Shelby (R-AL), then a member of the Senate Select Intelligence Committee. His words were chilling: "We knew this was going to happen. We just didn't know when. We're gonna hunt 'em down like dogs. Cuz that's what they are."

There were some lighter moments, too. When I saw Joseph Lieberman (D-CT), who was Al Gore's running mate in 2000, I flagged down Kent Conrad's chief of staff Bob Van Heuvelen outside Capitol Police headquarters. (Van Heuvelen and other Conrad staffers came out periodically to check on us, making sure we were okay.)

"Get me Lieberman! Get me Lieberman!" I shouted. Bob stopped the Senator before he departed. I could see Bob talking animatedly, and I could see Lieberman looking over at me. Then he broke into a big grin and nodded. He would do the interview.

Afterward, I asked Van Heuvelen how he had managed to get Lieberman, one of the "get" interviews at the time, to talk to me. I was surrounded by national media people. I was a bohunk from North Dakota broadcasting with a cell phone. And I got the interview.

Van Heuvelen explained, "I said, 'See that big redheaded guy over there? That's Ed Schultz. The most listened-to talk show host in North Dakota. If you had talked to him during the campaign, you would have carried North Dakota and won the election.'" Lieberman had no more answers than anyone that day. The death toll was nearly 3,000.

The last time America had lost so many lives in one day was on June 6, 1944—D Day, when an estimated 2,500 Americans died in the sand at Normandy, about the same number lost at Pearl Harbor on December 7, 1941. Instantly, Americans compared September 11 to the Japanese sneak attack. They grasped for parallels that weren't there. In 1941, it was one navy attacking another. (Hawaii was not yet even a state.) These were terrorists. Warfare had changed.

That evening, with the smoke from the Pentagon still in the air, Senators Byron Dorgan, Kent Conrad, and Representative Earl Pomeroy joined me for a special two-hour broadcast to my regional network in the Dakotas. Even back home, panic had set in. Rumors of gas shortages spread. Long lines at gas stations extended into the streets. Some stations raised prices, gouging customers. I think the broadcast helped calm North Dakotans. I know it made me feel better. It just helped to talk.

My admiration for Dorgan, Conrad, and Pomeroy's grace under pressure is tempered by my own guilt. For years, as a conservative talk show host, I had leveled brutal attacks against these men. Before my epiphany, I had gone as low as calling them *The Three Stooges.* To their credit, they never tried to retaliate. They treated me like a gentleman. They turned the other cheek so many times, I probably gave them whiplash.

Although we feel isolated in North Dakota, everyone seemed to know someone who had been in New York or Washington during the attack. Ann Nicole Nelson was the lone North Dakotan killed at the World Trade Center. She was a thirty-year-old employee of Cantor Fitzgerald on the 104th floor of the North Tower. She didn't have a chance. She was one of 658 employees lost by that company. A North Dakota town of about 1,200 residents was devastated. Minot State University named a building after her. I think it's easy to lose sight of the fact that for every one of those 3,000 people lost, whole families were shattered.

Hop-scotching across the country on Air Force One after cutting short a visit to a Florida classroom, President Bush was back in Washington shortly before 7 P.M. He spoke to the nation at 8:30 P.M. I thought he looked shaky—much more human than I wanted him to be in that moment. We needed a hero. We needed him. I wondered how Al Gore felt that day—if he looked up at the sky and said, "Thank God, it's not me," or if it gnawed at him that he could not be in the fight.

Did anyone in America sleep that night? As I lay in bed, staring at the ceiling and listening to the echo of sirens, I did not believe I could ever close my eyes again. I felt drained, wounded, like damaged goods. The world was a more uncertain place than it had ever been before.

But the sun came up in the morning. Sometime during the night, my eyes had closed. Like every other American, as I blinked at the morning light, I hoped it had been nothing more than a very bad dream. The pit in my stomach told me otherwise. I had changed. America had changed. Laurie Boeder had been right. *Everything* changed. The nightmare was real.

I am not afraid to say that, in the days after 9/11, I supported my president.

I cannot say that now.

The President
Lost Our Trust

C rucial to the integrity of the First Pillar—Defending the Nation—is trust. A nation must be able to trust its leaders to do the right thing. Franklin Delano Roosevelt took decisive actions, but just as important, he explained what he was doing in fireside chats on the radio. A great leader must be a great communicator. He must be an even better listener.

My father told me one day, "You can learn more by listening than by talking." This, to a future talk show host! But I've never forgotten the lesson. I think I do a pretty good job of listening to my callers.

All fathers have something to teach. I'd like to think I've passed on a nugget of wisdom now and then. It astounds me today that my president never benefited from the lessons his father learned in the first Gulf War. George H. W. Bush and former National Security Advisor Brent Scowcroft wrote in *Time* magazine in 1998: "Extending the war into Iraq [in 1991] would have incurred incalculable human and political costs. We would have been forced to occupy Baghdad and, in effect, rule Iraq. The coalition would instantly have collapsed, the Arabs deserting in anger and other allies pulling out as well. Exceeding the U.N.'s mandate would have destroyed the precedent of international response to aggression we hoped to establish. Had we gone the invasion route, the U.S. could still be an occupying power in a bitterly hostile land."

The old man had it right.

What we lost as a country on September 11 pales in comparison to what we gained on September 12. On September 12, 2001, most of the world lined up behind us! Gee whiz, Republicans and Democrats even started speaking to each other again! They sang *God Bless America* together on the Capitol steps! Adversity had united us! Democrats supported the war in Afghanistan, and the world supported *us*. How do you screw *that* up?

Well, it starts with geography. You gotta know the difference between Afghanistan and Iraq. Former Senator Gary Hart said in a *Boston Globe* opinion piece (June 2, 2003),

> The war on terrorism morphed into the centerpiece of a new imperial foreign policy. Consequences abound. A nation whose announced national security policy is to eradicate dictators possessing weapons is then immediately faced with North Korea. Indeed, we are faced with a good number of nations fitting this description. Either we mean what we say, or we pick and choose. And if we pick and choose, what standards do we use? Whom do we invade and with whom do we negotiate? And if we can adopt this preemptive policy, why cannot other nations? You can either believe much of the rest of the world became, almost overnight, obtuse and anti-American, or you can more plausibly believe we unilaterally launched ourselves on a mission that made little sense to the rest of the world.

Today, I am a citizen in a country ostracized by world opinion. We have lost faith in our leaders. The world has lost faith in us. Our foray into Iraq to disarm a nation of biological and nuclear weapons they did not have has shrunk American credibility like a cheap sweater. I live in a country polarized—in a world we have polarized.

It all started with such promise.

I was inspired the night of September 20, 2001, by a president who delivered one of the greatest speeches in this country's history before a joint session of Congress and the world:

> Tonight, we are a country awakened to danger and called to defend freedom. Our grief has been turned to anger and anger to resolution. Whether we bring our enemies to justice or bring justice to our enemies, justice will be done.

It was powerful. George W. Bush had it all. I wanted the president to succeed! I hadn't voted for him, but I sure supported him.

Just months after 9/11, Wendy and I were invited to the 2002 State of the Union address. It was a special moment for me. When I was growing up in Norfolk, Virginia, my parents listened closely to what the president said during the State of the Union address. As an aeronautical engineer employed by the government, my father paid close attention to military budgets. When the president delivered a State of the Union address, it was like the Super Bowl for him. I grew up knowing that when the president speaks, it's the playbook—the road map—for the country.

Even though my politics had changed some years back, I did not come to Washington as a cynic. I'm a patriotic American! This was a huge honor—something my father would have given his eyeteeth to do. I came to continue my support for what I thought at the time was *very good leadership.*

That's why it angers me when my love for America is trivialized and misrepresented by the neocon hatchet jobs and the lie that

Democrats cheer when things go wrong in this country. *All* Americans want what is best for America! We're not suicidal.

Today, when I look back on that State of the Union Speech, I am deeply disappointed that my president has fallen so far short of the goals he laid out that night. He said,

> Once we have funded our national security and our homeland security, the final great priority of my budget is economic security for the American people. To achieve these great national objectives—to win the war, protect the homeland, and revitalize our economy—our budget will run a deficit that will be small and short-term, so long as Congress restrains spending and acts in a fiscally responsible manner.

Let's break it down, homeland security first. Port security in the proposed budget has been cut 63 percent to $46 million. The Coast Guard says it would cost $500 million more to adequately secure our nation's 361 seaports. A nuclear weapon detonated in a cargo container would wipe out a city. Only 4 percent of such containers are inspected. The new budget dedicates no specific resources to protect the nation's 104 nuclear power plants and 120 chemical plants. Let's at least issue some pepper spray!

In North Dakota, our border with Canada is sometimes defended by nothing more than orange cones in the middle of the road. We had better hope no one is smuggling in anything more than Moosehead Beer and Cuban cigars. Oh, well, It's just North Dakota, right? It's a state with two air bases. There are energy plants. There's also a big dam at Garrison that, if blown up, would flood cities along the Missouri River. And it's a state with free access to the rest of the United States!

Minnesota, which also shares a border with Canada, has two nuclear plants within thirty miles of Minneapolis. Do you know who lives in Minneapolis? Prince! I am willing to make some concessions for homeland security. I am not willing to sacrifice the funk.

The gap between agents on the northern border is *five and a half miles*. Our southern border is patrolled by five agents per mile. And we know how well *that* is going.

The 2005 budget slashes the Nunn-Lugar Cooperative Threat Reduction Program, which helps track and contain loose nuclear material around the globe. This key element in protecting America from the mushroom cloud that our administration warned us about on the eve of the invasion of Iraq, has been under-funded by 9 percent—$42 million. That worries me.

Americans signed on for the war in Afghanistan because they wanted Osama bin Laden brought to justice. Dead or alive. But they wanted to be more secure, too. They understood that the war on terror, first and foremost, demanded better protection at home. This has got to be the first priority.

Iraq was the wrong step at the wrong time. If we didn't know it then, we can be sure of it now. We can't afford homeland security because we're giving tax cuts to the rich and shouldering 90 percent of the bills and manpower in Iraq!

Today, we may well have a coalition of the *willing*.

We sure don't have a coalition of the *giving*.

In 1991, America's share of the first Gulf War was $13 billion. Our own administration has placed the price tag on this one at $200 billion, and when you consider their dyslexic accounting practices, you have to double that. The only way I can get a handle on what the administration is telling me is to double every figure they give me, except job creation projections, which I divide by five. In all other instances, I just assume they'll do the exact opposite of what they tell me.

I'm a uniter not a divider. *Oops.*

My plan reduces the national debt. *Oops.*

We know Iraq has weapons of mass destruction. *Oops.*

We're not going to nation-build. *Oops.*

We'll be welcomed by the Iraqis. *Oops.*

Mission accomplished. *Big oops.*

Connect the dots.

Americans don't want condescension and platitudes. We know a mistake when we see one. But the president acts like he ate a lemon if you ask him a question about it. He forgets that we don't work for *him.* He works for *us.* With the job comes accountability. I compare it to my playing days. When I walked off the field after throwing a stupid interception, my coach would pull me aside and ask me, "What the hell happened?" Sometimes I might explain that the receiver ran the wrong route or that I misjudged the coverage. Lots of times I just confessed, "I screwed up. I'm a bonehead." My coach just wanted to know that *I understood* I had botched the job. That way he could be reasonably certain I wouldn't make the same mistake again. That's all the American people want from this administration. A little reassurance. Instead, Bush is flipping us the bird and Cheney is mooning us from the back seat.

I am tired of being preached to by the radio righties and the Bushies about what message it sends to our soldiers in Iraq when we question where this administration is taking us and how many more young Americans will get thrown into the meat grinder. We're paying a high price in lives and in dollars. I want to know, Mr. President, what message it sends to our soldiers when your 2005 budget slashes veterans' benefits by $521 million. It's a big "screw you" to the American soldier. It is the height of hypocrisy to talk about supporting America's soldiers at a time when 200,000 of them from Desert Storm are suffering from Gulf War Syndrome, an illness *still* not recognized by the Department of Defense.

Take the case of Kevin Shores, a St. Paul, Minnesota, native. Kevin was the first guy who called my show to tell me about Gulf War Syndrome. *The High Plains Reader* of Fargo later did a great story on him:

> When Kevin Shores enlisted in the Navy in the summer of 1985, he was 5 feet, 11 inches tall and weighed 185 pounds. Shores was an active young man, captain of his high school swim team, and an ambitious young sailor. He was raised in a military family. His father and grandfather had both served, and he was eager to carry on that legacy. Today, pain engulfs Shores' daily life. He now weighs less than 145 pounds, has no cartilage in his joints (which have solidified with calcium deposits), and his once athletic build has deteriorated to a physical structure confined to an electric wheelchair. Every moment hurts, every task is burdensome.

Shores says, "I remember it was like walking on needles every step. In '92 I used to have a regimen. I'd wake up every morning—this is in the winter. I would fill up the bathtub with about six inches of freezing water. I would turn the cold water on and let that fill up the bathtub. I would step into the bathtub and I would turn on the hot shower on the rest of my body. This was one of the only ways to alleviate the pain I felt." After walking with a cane for a while, Shores soon needed two crutches, and by 1994 the Veterns' Administration (VA) gave him a wheelchair to which he is still confined.

The cause? He's been getting the runaround from the VA.

In the *High Plains Reader* story, Shores said, "The very first thing they started telling sick vets was that the sand was so fine in the Middle East that Americans weren't used to breathing in the fine sand. And then they were telling us there were mites in the sand, and that the mites were biting us and giving us these sicknesses. Then they were telling us that Saddam was using biological and chemical weapons on us. Then, there were rumors that *we* were using biological and chemical weapons. And the very last thing being talked about was experimental inoculations [given to the troops before the war]."

The 1994 Senate Riegle Report says chemical and biological weapons were used in the war. Staff Sergeant Willie Hicks testified about what he believes was a chemical attack: "It was around 2:30 in the morning. The chemical alarms went off. As we were running to the bunker, we started burning. Our faces were burning. Some guys just dropped. . . . About two or three days later, a couple of guys started getting sick. I got sick myself. I had discharge with my urine with blood in it. The Commanding Officer put out an order that nobody would discuss it. . . . 85 of the 110 guys who came back with the unit were sick. . . . Staff Sergeant Neal is now nothing more than a vegetable. . . . I carry notebooks all the time now because my memory is gone. I used to teach school. I had to quit my job because I kept passing out or getting lost going to work. . . . I went from 170 to 126 [pounds] last month. . . . I have no income. I lost my car. I was getting desperate for funds to support my family with. The VA tried to charge me $169 a day for being in the hospital. I went up and questioned it. I said, 'This is service connected.' The lady said you have not proven it to be service connected, therefore, we are charging you $169 a day. I said, 'I have no income.' She said, 'it makes no difference.' I am also a veteran from the Vietnam War. I think this is Vietnam all over again because I know how I was treated when I came back from there. . . . I have been completely forgotten. And I am sick and unable to work because I served my country."

I have a special spot in my heart for Vietnam veterans after an experience I had on Veterans Day, 2002. I took the Big Eddie Cruiser to the Fargo Air Museum where an area nursing home was bringing veterans that day. I wanted to talk to these old World War II B-17 and B-24 bomber pilots. While I was doing the program, I saw a group of men I later discovered were Vietnam veterans. I was really struck by the fact that they didn't want to talk about Vietnam—they were *ashamed* to have fought in Vietnam. They had been so beaten down, and they were never given any respect. My heart really went out to these guys. *Set the politics aside.* These guys had nothing to do with that. They stepped to the plate when they were called.

I'm really proud of what transpired after that show. Toby McPherson, the pilot who saved my show, is on the board of directors of the Fargo Air Museum. He and his fellow directors decided to hold Vietnam Week at the museum the following spring. It's been a huge success. In Spring 2004, 11,000 people went through the gates in one week to see what is regarded as one of the best displays of Vietnam War memorabilia in the country. Toby says it's going to get bigger every year. "There's so much interest—so much support," he says. One man I had on *The Ed Schultz Show* is Vietnam veteran John Hovde, a double amputee, who has gone to speak at area schools in conjunction with Vietnam Week. John, who soon plans to have a book out about his experiences, told Toby he was motivated by something he saw in a history book. "For a war that lasted sixteen years," he said, "Vietnam merited only three pages."

When I did a broadcast during Vietnam Week, the veterans were typically reluctant to talk. But finally, one told his story, then another . . . and another. It was a catharsis. Some of these guys had never spoken about the war to *anybody.* I think it helped to talk. It helped to know that on radios across the Upper Midwest, people were listening and caring.

During the broadcast, somebody mentioned that Ron Sahr, a former Fargo city councilman, had been in Vietnam. I called Ron at his gas station, Sahr's Sudden Service, and asked him if he'd go on the air with me. He agreed, and for the first time ever, he talked about being a medic in Vietnam. We had been friends, fished together, and he had never once talked about those harrowing experiences. Vietnam was something you just didn't talk about. I think it's a shame that we have a generation of soldiers who feel so maligned.

Good things often spring from the shows I take on the road. There are stories like this in every town—in your town. Maybe you ought to look for a way to honor your Vietnam veterans. I'm so pleased to have played a small part in seeing that these great men are appreciated. It makes me angry when I hear about veterans dying of cancer from the Agent Orange defoliant used in Vietnam, and being denied full benefits.

One day, I got a call from a listener who told me about the U.S. military using radioactive ammunition. It seemed far-fetched. It wasn't. After reading an August 4, 2003, story from Larry Johnson, a reporter in Baghdad for the *Seattle Post-Intelligencer,* I wondered if radiation wasn't at least partially responsible for Gulf War Syndrome.

Johnson writes, "Some Iraqi physicians and others blame depleted uranium weapons used in the 1991 Gulf War for a major increase of cancers and birth defects that occurred a few years later. It is also a prime suspect for the Gulf War Syndrome that has sickened and killed thousands of U.S. veterans. The Pentagon and United Nations estimate that U.S. and British forces used 1,100 to 2,000 tons of armor-piercing shells made of depleted uranium in the 1991 Gulf War. U.S. tanks, Bradley fighting machines, A-10 attack jets and Apache helicopters routinely used depleted uranium rounds, but in the recent war, the ammunition was used in and near heavily populated areas, not just in the desert."

Rep. Jim McDermott (D-WA), who is quoted in the story, has introduced legislation to conduct studies of depleted uranium's effects on health and the environment, and cleanup of DU contamination in America. He said, "We continue to get these sporadic reports of various places where a lot of people are getting sick (including birth defects), and nobody is willing to connect the dots yet. I'm afraid we're going to have a lot of people get sick before they finally admit that depleted uranium really causes a problem for us (U.S. veterans and their families) as well as for the Iraqis."

The story goes on to quote an independent policy analyst on the use and effects of DU. The report was critical of both the British and the Americans for not doing more to protect their troops and civilians from DU in Iraq. But the report held criticism for those on all sides of the DU issue. "What is clear . . . is that elements of the U.S. government will manipulate information and even lie about the health of U.S. combat veterans to avoid liability for DU's health and environmental effects," said Dan Fahey, who has testified on DU at a number of congressional hearings.

While Johnson's story warns that anti-DU activists might be spreading disinformation, my gut tells me that when they sort it all out, the American soldier will find he has been terribly abused, as happened with so many Vietnam veterans.

What's next? Do we do what MacArthur did in 1932 when he was ordered to drive 25,000 penniless World War I veterans out of Washington, D.C., for having the temerity to ask Congress for help? MacArthur and his soldiers burned tents and forcibly removed the veterans and their families from their makeshift encampments near the Capitol when the veterans asked the government for an early payout of agreed-upon bonuses. The soldiers wanted loyalty from their government. The Hoover administration didn't give it to them. Neither does this one.

This same administration even wanted to roll back 2003 pay increases—combat pay and separation allowances for family expenses back home—for the soldiers fighting the battles in Iraq and Afghanistan. Howard Dean pointed out, "Cheney will reap a $116,000 per year tax windfall, and yet our soldiers—on extended deployments and tragically dying every day—are facing pay cuts of $225 a month."

If the First Pillar of Defense is to be solid, we have to have the loyalty of the American soldier. But in order to get loyalty, we have to offer it in return. These people deserve better. They have sacrificed beyond measure.

Senator John McCain (R-AZ) had it right when he said that cutting taxes during wartime showed a lack of sacrifice. Republican Speaker of the House Dennis Hastert (R-IL) immediately blasted McCain for straying from the "company" line. Hastert suggested to McCain, a former POW, that he visit the wounded soldiers if he wanted to see sacrifice. McCain responded, "I agree with Hastert that these young men and women are making enormous sacrifices and I have visited them. But I think we owe them something else and that is not to come back to a bankrupt nation. I'm a loyal Republican. We are now on the biggest spending, tax-cutting binge we've ever been in history and we're doing terrible things to the future of this country." McCain is right. We're sending them off to hell and bringing them home to a country in economic tatters.

The whopper our president told us in the 2002 State of the Union Address is, "Our budget will run a deficit that will be small and short term." He *knew* better. Even then, he had a boondoggle of a Medicare Prescription Bill in the works to the tune of

$540 billion—$140 billion more than he said it would cost. Even during the State of the Union, the president was making a case for an Axis of Bankruptcy with an expensive and untimely war in Iraq. It was full speed ahead with the tax cuts, full speed ahead with record deficits, and a record debt. The $318 billion we pay on *interest* on the national debt each year would fund veteran's benefits. It would pay for a lot of homeland security. But run along home with your duct tape and plastic sheeting, they tell us.

The Herd Mentality

I f the president's failures of leadership eroded the First Pillar—Defending the Nation, then the right wing's orchestrated lies, half-truths, and propaganda have put a jackhammer to it and freedom itself.

Americans got stampeded.

The landscape of the Great Plains I see every day was once covered with millions of buffalo. These buffalo are what sustained the American Indians—the Sioux, Crow, and Cheyenne. The buffalo provided food, clothing, and tools. It is said, quite accurately, that there was a use for every part of the buffalo. The Indians were free until the buffalo were nearly killed off at the hands of the white hunters who invaded Indian lands. It's not characterized as an *invasion* in the history books. Indeed, some well-meaning whites saw an opportunity to "civilize the heathens." Just who required the civilizing depends on whom you ask.

Ann Coulter's take on Muslim extremists is proof that this mind-set is still with us today: "We should invade their countries, kill their leaders, and convert them to Christianity. We weren't punctilious about locating and punishing only Hitler and his top officers. We carpet-bombed German cities; we killed civilians. That's war. And this is war." I think she has rabies. Did you know if you hold her head to your ear, you can hear the sound of the ocean?

But back to my buffalo analogy.

While buffalo hunt scenes like the one in *Dances with Wolves* did play out, a common hunting tactic was to stampede them to a pre-selected spot. Thousands of frightened buffalo ran like hell. Only those in the front had any sense of the terrain ahead. By the time the front-runners realized what lay ahead—*a cliff*—it was too late. They were pushed over the precipice and buried beneath the other falling bodies.

Now look at what happened to Americans in the run-up to the Iraq War. We *thought* we were the hunters, but it turned out we were the buffalo.

The plan to go into Iraq was brewing long before President George W. Bush was elected. The rightie squawking heads (because they parrot the same message) and the administration have pulled the wool over our eyes. Many Americans remain convinced Saddam was connected to 9/11. The administration has not gone out of its way to change the notion. Let's put the pieces together.

A nation must have the *political will* to fight a war. If you go back to the booming economy of the Clinton era with everyone lined up at the Wall Street trough, did America have the political will to seriously fight the war on terror? I don't think so. Bill Clinton should be held accountable for some security failures—if you're going to Monday morning quarterback it. He *did* order an unsuccessful cruise missile attack on bin Laden in 1998, however. Even then, Clinton was criticized for supposedly trying to distract the public eye from the Lewinsky scandal.

After the October 2000 bombing of the U.S.S. *Cole* in a Yemen port, antiterrorism czar Richard Clarke advocated an attack on terrorist training camps in Afghanistan that never happened. At least, the Clinton administration tried to get the incoming Bush administration to focus on terrorism. But the Bush administration didn't listen until it was too late.

A little over a month before 9/11, on August 6, 2001, President Bush's daily briefing memo was entitled, "Bin Laden Determined to Strike in U.S." The memo said that bin Laden's followers might be planning to hijack U.S. airliners. The president took no action.

Though we have the newly formed Department of Homeland Security, there seems to be a turf war between Homeland Security Director Tom Ridge and Attorney General John Ashcroft. This was never more obvious than on the eve of Memorial Day weekend of 2004, when Ridge held a press conference to ease people's fears about travel during the holiday. Ashcroft followed with a dire warning that al Qaeda plans for an attack were 90 percent complete. The administration's messages are increasingly fragmented and contradictory. While the president admits there was no Iraq–al Qaeda connection, Dick Cheney continues to insist to this day that there was.

Before the 2000 election, the neocon think tank, Project for the New American Century, issued a treatise on defense entitled, "Rebuilding America's Defenses." The paper advocates an expanded military able to fight simultaneous, multiple wars. The report says, "The process of transformation, even if it brings revolutionary change, is likely to be a long one, absent some catastrophic and catalyzing event—like a new Pearl Harbor." This came on the heels of a 1998 letter in which the think tank urged President Bill Clinton and key Republican leaders for "the removal of Saddam Hussein's regime from power." Of the eighteen people who signed the letter, ten are now in the Bush administration. They include Defense Secretary Donald Rumsfeld, his deputy Paul Wolfowitz, Deputy Secretary of State Richard Armitage, Zalmay Khalilzad, the White House liaison to the

Iraqi opposition, and Richard Perle, former chairman of an influential Pentagon advisory board. As further proof of this administration's obsession with toppling Saddam, note the central topic of its second National Security Council meeting on February 1, 2001: "Plan for Post-Saddam Iraq."

It's a bad recipe—you've got a disengaged, weak president surrounded by extremists with an agenda. After 9/11, they believed they had the excuse they needed to go after Iraq. Rumsfeld urged the bombing of Iraq the next day. Anti-terrorism czar Richard Clarke told *60 Minutes,* "We all said . . . no, no. Al Qaeda is in Afghanistan. We need to bomb Afghanistan. And Rumsfeld said there aren't any good targets in Afghanistan. And there are lots of good targets in Iraq. I said, 'Well, there are lots of good targets in lots of places, but Iraq had nothing to do with it.'"

It reminds me of the man who was looking for his watch under the street lamp.

"But, I thought you lost it in the alley," his friend said.

"I did," the man said. "But the light is better here."

The neocons recognized 9/11 as the "Pearl Harbor" they were waiting for. Even though the pieces didn't fit, they resolved to *make* them fit to justify a war against Iraq. They fear-mongered and misinformed. It was a betrayal of the American people. Americans supported a war on terrorism. Damn right they wanted to hunt bin Laden down! We had the support of many nations. There was unprecedented cooperation among intelligence-gathering organizations in these countries. We squandered all that goodwill by artificially building a case for war in Iraq.

It was an orchestrated sales job that had its roots in a neocon think tank that thought the first President Bush had erred by not finishing the job in Iraq. Of course, he was bound by an agreement from the coalition not to occupy Iraq. Bush believed that Saddam was sufficiently weakened to pave the way for an overthrow. He was wrong. Bill Clinton had it right in one respect. Militarily, he had Saddam contained.

The specific justifications the administration made for war—weapons of mass destruction and a connection to al Qaeda—proved false. So how does the administration respond? They create *new* justifications for the war, *after the fact.* And they're trying to convince us that they said it all along. It's more than spin; it's an attempt to revise history. The new explanation is that we just wanted to liberate Iraq: "Hi, we were in the neighborhood and thought we'd drop in to shock and awe you." Okay, let me get this straight. All of a sudden Dick Cheney is a humanitarian?

Look, I think liberating the people of Iraq from Saddam Hussein is a noble by-product of this war. How can you argue that? But liberating Iraq was never the case for war. The case for war was: *We have to get Saddam before he gets us.* Americans who supported the war bought the argument that there was an *imminent* threat. Otherwise, they would have proceeded at a much more cautious pace to change leadership in Iraq. Americans were sold one bill of goods and got another. Never was Saddam's abuse of his people an argument for war. It was an aside. If it really was a rescue mission with a human rights agenda, then George H. W. Bush should have invaded China after Tiananmen Square in 1989.

Defense requires accurate intelligence. The Bush administration was so intent on making a case for war, they fell for stories from Iraqis in exile who had a *vested interest* in Saddam's overthrow. There were some huge question marks about the legitimacy of the information. It cost them credibility.

Colin Powell was the only one in the administration with the credibility to make the case for war to the United Nations, and they used him. Fifteen and a half months after his speech to the United

Nations, Powell backtracked. On *Meet the Press,* he said, "At the time that I made the presentation, it reflected the collective judgment, the sound judgment of the intelligence community. But it turned out that the sourcing was inaccurate and wrong and in some cases, deliberately misleading. And for that, I am disappointed and I regret it." Consider the definition of those two words: Deliberately misleading.

It means *lie.*

In a 2001 *PBS Frontline* program, Richard Perle, the leading proponent for war, said, "I think there would be dancing in the streets if Saddam were removed from power, and that reaction of the Iraqi people would be reflected in the attitude of the Arab world, generally. So the notion that if we go after Iraq we are somehow going to advance in the direction of a war against Islam that will turn out far worse for us, I think is really quite mistaken. . . ."

Dancing in the streets? Only around the bodies of dead Americans.

Bush and the neocons created a climate in which they pushed so hard to make a case for the war in Iraq, underlings felt obligated to give them what they wanted. Richard Clarke recounted on *60 Minutes* what happened after 9/11. "The president dragged me into a room with a couple of other people, shut the door, and said, 'I want you to find whether Iraq did this.' Now he never said, 'Make it up.' But the entire conversation left me in absolutely no doubt that George Bush wanted me to come back with a report that said Iraq did this. I said, 'Mr. President. We've done this before. We have been looking at this. We looked at it with an open mind. There's no connection.'

"He came back at me and said, 'Iraq! Saddam! Find out if there's a connection.' And in a very intimidating way."

Resigned CIA Director George Tenet told the president *exactly* what he wanted to hear when he called Saddam's alleged possession of weapons of mass destruction (WMDs) a "slam dunk."

I was there when George Bush's case for war and a preemptive strike began to emerge in the 2002 "Axis of Evil" State of the Union Address. Everyone in the administration followed suit. "Simply stated, there is *no doubt* that Saddam Hussein now has weapons of mass destruction," Dick Cheney said.

On October 7, 2002, Bush said Saddam "must not be permitted to threaten America and the world with horrible poisons and diseases and atomic weapons." The height of hypocrisy was when the righties declared we had to disarm Saddam of the very weapons we were duplicitous in creating. Conservative columnist William Safire wrote in 1992, "Iraqgate is uniquely horrendous: a scandal about the systematic abuse of power by misguided leaders of three democratic nations (the United States, Britain, and Italy) to secretly finance the arms buildup of a dictator."

We know Rumsfeld and the rest of the Reagan administration looked the other way when Saddam used chemical weapons against Iran, but we don't know the depths of Bush I's involvement. Bush II has taken secrecy to new levels. He embargoed Ronald Reagan's presidential papers previously cleared by Reagan's library staff, overriding Reagan's wishes that they be released twelve years after he left office.

Bush said it was for national security. Helen Thomas, in a column for Hearst Newspapers, wrote, "The order is clearly protective of the president's father and officials who are back at the White House in top jobs after serving in the Bush I administration between 1989 and 1993." She adds, "Secrecy is endemic in government, but this order goes counter to the American tradition of government by the people and for the people. . . . Is the Bush White House trying to protect the reputations of prominent political players—especially George H. W. Bush—through the suppression of historic data? If so, that would deny the American people a chance to hold past public servants accountable, albeit belatedly." In 2001, eight million documents were classified secret. In 2003, fourteen million were classified secret.

After 9/11, the call to attack Iraq was everywhere. Even former Secretary of State George Schultz got into the act in an opinion column for the *Washington Post* a year after 9/11:

Self-defense is a valid basis for preemptive action. The evidence is clear that Hussein continues to amass weapons of mass destruction. . . . By now, the risks of inaction clearly outweigh the risks of action. If there is a rattlesnake in the yard, you don't wait for it to strike before you take action in self-defense.

The sales job on the American people had begun.

So here we are today—at a crossroads. The question is: Where do we go from here? Some days I feel like we're hurtling toward oblivion with the neocons shouting in our ears, "Stay the course!"

Clearly, America has to clean up the mess in Iraq. Whether it is John Kerry or George Bush in the White House, America has an obligation to correct our wrongs. It won't happen quickly. Even the Bush administration has started to publicly acknowledge that. In June 2004, on the eve of the transfer of power to a new Iraqi government, Colin Powell warned of a "hot, bloody summer."

Rightie talk show host Laura Ingraham bristled at the notion during an interview on Bill O'Reilly's *No Spin Zone* on June 14, 2004. She said the administration needed to put a more "positive spin" on the situation. O'Reilly argued—*correctly*—that by continuing to paint a rosy picture, the administration stood to lose credibility. Ingraham also complained that many television news anchors, including *Fox*'s Brit Hume, in a lapse into objectivity, had led with a story of bombings in Iraq.

Analyze that. Ingraham wants a more "positive spin" from the administration and for the media to go easy on bad news. In short, she wants to *manage the news.* It's not about objectivity; it's about an agenda. The righties want to make sure you hear only what they want you to hear. They don't trust the American people with the truth.

Remember the buffalo.

They're trying to stampede you again.

In the decades to come, American soldiers and the American taxpayer will pay for America's headlong rush into Iraq. I hope the Iraqis appreciate what we're doing for them. I really do. If we can leave them with a stable government, much good will have come from our mistake. As we dig out of the hole in Iraq, Americans need to take a good hard look at the Bush doctrine of preemptive strikes. The neocons seem intent on wading deeper into the quicksand.

Richard Perle, in his 2004 book *An End to Evil: How to Win the War of Terror,* co-authored by former Bush speechwriter David Frum, makes a shrill case for the Bush doctrine: "[A] radical strain within Islam seeks to overthrow our civilization and remake the nations of the West into Islamic societies, imposing on the whole world, its religion and laws."

In his review of the book in the *American Conservative,* Patrick Buchanan points out that agenda has been on the table since the seventh century, and in the past twenty-five years, militant Islam has managed to seize just three countries: Iran, Sudan, and Afghanistan. Iran shows signs of becoming more moderate. Afghanistan fell without much of a fight, and the Sudan remains a weak nation, still recovering from years of civil war.

Buchanan says, "Wherever Islaminism takes power, it fails. Like Marxism, it does not work." Terrorists resort to terror, he says, because it is the only weapon they have. He does not downplay the threat of dirty bombs and terror attacks on soft targets but says, "As in the Cold War, time is on America's side. Perseverance and patience are called for, not this panic."

Buchanan says, "Fear is what Perle and his co-author David Frum are peddling to stampede America into serial wars. Just such fear-mongering got us into Iraq. . . . Iraq was never the clear and present danger the authors insist she was."

Perle and Frum, the author of Bush's "Axis of Evil" speech, call for the overthrow of Iran, a country three times as large and populous as Iraq. Syria is on the list. And North Korea. And Saudi Arabia is seeing the fruits of the terrorism seeds it planted in its home soil. The CATO Institute, a conservative think tank, said in 2001:

> The Saudi monarchy has funded dubious schools and "charities" throughout the Islamic world. Those organizations have been hotbeds of anti-Western, and especially, anti-American indoctrination. The schools, for example, not only indoctrinate students in a virulent and extreme form of Islam, but also teach them to hate secular Western values. They are also taught that the United States is the center of infidel power in the world and is the enemy of Islam. Graduates of those schools are frequently recruits for Bin Laden's al-Qaeda terror network as well as other extremist groups.

Attack Saudi Arabia? It's a red herring. Our dependence on Saudi Arabia to manipulate world oil prices, buy American weapons (they're our largest customer), and invest in America prohibits any dissolution of the alliance anytime soon. Then, there are those curious Bush family/bin Laden family connections. . . . *And the fact that planeloads of Osama's relatives were spirited out of America two days after 9/11 by the U.S. government. It is astonishing to me that there has been no real media coverage on this issue, no congressional inquiry*—nothing. The story exists in the shadows.

Interestingly, George H. W. Bush was in a meeting of the Carlyle Group with one of bin Laden's brothers at the Ritz-Carlton in Washington, D.C., on 9/11. With its defense industry holdings, the Carlyle Group owns 50 percent of United Technologies. They make Bradley armored vehicles, missile systems, and much more. It is the largest private equity manager in the world, valued at $18 billion, according to *Bloomberg News*. The Carlyle Group has a heady cast of players that include James Baker III, Bush senior's secretary of state, and John Major, the former prime minister of Great Britain. Bush Senior and Baker are listed as advisors. We know that George W. Bush was once on the board of one of the Carlyle Group's holdings, Caterair, an airline food service, which he left before becoming governor of Texas in 1992.

What did it all mean? Was it just the global rich consorting with the global rich? I couldn't draw a concrete conclusion. Was I the only one asking these questions? Turns out, I wasn't. Two weeks before this manuscript was to be turned into the publisher, Wendy and I went to see *Fahrenheit 9/11,* in which Michael Moore asks the same questions.

Today, the Carlyle Group, a company that benefits greatly from arms sales, has direct connections to the White House. *You think father and son don't talk?* The people making the decisions to go to war are intertwined with the people who benefit from war. Is the defense industry running foreign policy? It's high time the American people got some answers.

And what about the president's ties to Saudi Arabia? His old National Guard buddy, Jim Bath, has allegedly been a conduit for Saudi money. In Bob McKeown's interview with Charles W. White, Bath's former partner, which aired on October 29, 2003 as part of a Canadian Broadcast Corporation program, White said:

> Bath explained to me that he had been tapped by George Senior to set up a quasi-private aircraft firm that would basically engage in CIA-sponsored activities funded by the Saudi Royal Family. He explained that the Saudis had basically entered into a quid pro quo relationship with Bush and that Bush, when he was CIA Director, worked with the head of Saudi Intelligence and the CIA trained the Palace Guard to protect the Saudi Royal Family who was concerned about a fundamentalist revolution. And it was at that point I think that this thing got kicked into high gear and the Saudis agreed to provide surreptitious funding to the United States to fight its secret wars in Afghanistan and Nicaragua. Payback came when Bush as Vice President sent AWACS and F-15 fighter jets to Saudi Arabia and supported Saddam Hussein under the adage that "the enemy of my enemy is my friend." We had the Iran-Iraq War at the time so that's really how the relationship evolved.

White believes the bin Laden family invested $1 million in Bush Jr.'s fledgling Arbusto (which means "bush" in Spanish) company in 1979. When the company floundered, White says:

> Bush's Saudi friends were there to bail him out: . . . Arbusto went through several iterations and became Harken Energy. My understanding is that once again the Arabs came in and bailed Bush Jr. out of some bad business ventures resulting from his bad business decisions and that because of this, he was able to cash in his chips prematurely before the stock nose-dived.

Many Americans are beginning to wonder just how hog-tied George W. Bush is by his Saudi connections. White goes on to say,

> I can't help wondering if the money that changed hands back during my experiences with Bath hasn't influenced or clouded or even compromised the president's ability to wage war against terrorism. I just can't imagine how he can be an objective arbitrator of the bin Laden family's activities when in fact he's taken money from them that's never been reported publicly. I think he's compromised and that's of great concern to me. And I think that it's also a great concern to the families of the victims of the 9/11 tragedy.

We have to wonder why we have committed so few troops—about 20,000—to Afghanistan. And we have to wonder how badly the Bush administration wants a trial starring bin Laden with his family as witnesses. Dead or alive? *Nah, let's just invade Iraq. You know, distract the sheep. Er, I mean, Americans.*

The need to establish a foothold in Iraq, with the second largest known oil reserves in the world, becomes obvious when you consider the shaky state of Saudi Arabia, the country with the world's largest reserves. The country, ruled by a monarchy and dominated by an extremist Wahhabi sect, is entirely dependent on oil.

Forty percent of the population is under eighteen years old, fertile ground for Wahhabi extremism. Unemployment, officially at 30 percent, is probably much higher. Terrorists have begun targeting American oil workers in Saudi Arabia, vital to keeping the oil flowing and the monarchy entrenched. A coup is a real possibility. Even though the amount of oil that America gets from Saudi Arabia seems relatively insignificant—20 percent of our total use—if Saudi Arabia's ten to eleven million barrel-a-day production vanished from the market, gas prices in America could spike to five or six dollars a gallon, plummeting the country in a certain recession. Or worse. Connect the dots. The Iraq invasion was planned long before 9/11 as a way of hedging our bets in the Middle East.

"Oh, no," the administration has said time and time again. "It's not about oil!"

Translation: It's *all about oil!*

Richard Perle made a case for war with Iraq in a 2001 column about Khidir Hamza, "one of the people who ran the nuclear weapons program for Saddam." Perle cited Hamza's report of *400 uranium enrichment facilities.* Wow, you'd think we would have found *one* of them by now. Patrick Buchanan says, "Did Hamza deliberately deceive Perle or did Perle deliberately deceive us?" One wonders how far to the right Perle has to be to make Patrick Buchanan appear liberal in his position.

Perle was forced to resign as chairman of the Pentagon Defense Policy Board after disclosures of his business ties to a Saudi arms peddler and a consulting contract for a communications company seeking permission from the Defense Department to be sold to Chinese investors—a clear conflict of interest. Perle also failed to disclose financial ties to Boeing while pushing a Boeing bid for a $20-billion defense contract to lease and then buy one hundred modified refueling planes. This happened a year after Boeing committed to invest up to $20 million in a New York venture capital fund in which Perle is a major player. Coincidences abound.

The similarities between Perle and Cheney, the former CEO of Halliburton, are worth noting. The continuing connections between Cheney and Halliburton are still unraveling despite Cheney's public denials. He told Tim Russert he had severed all ties with the company, yet an e-mail from the Pentagon implicates Cheney's office in the coordination of a $7 billion contract between the Pentagon and Halliburton.

In 2000, Cheney acknowledged that Halliburton (through foreign subsidiaries) did business with "Axis of Evil" nations Libya and Iran. He denied dealing with Saddam Hussein, though. "Iraq's different," he said. The *Washington Post,* however, discovered that "Halliburton held stakes in two firms that signed contracts to sell more than $73 million in oil production equipment and spare parts." In a July 30, 2000 interview on ABC's *This Week* program, Cheney expressly denied that Halliburton or any of its subsidiaries did business with Iraq. He was forced to recant when the Iraq deals were made public.

Cheney, a guy who got the job at Halliburton because of the doors he could open to U.S. government contracts, got $30 million in parting gifts when he "left the company." Cheney has long been an enthusiastic supporter of privatizing just about everything the U.S. government does.

Halliburton was awarded the contract to rebuild Iraq's oil infrastructure by the Pentagon by circumventing the bid process. The bullet-point reply was that Halliburton was the only company capable of doing the job. I still remember one of my callers responding, "Yeah, well then they shouldn't have had any trouble winning the bid!"

It's about connections. The connection between the military, the government, and big business was a specter Dwight Eisenhower saw on the horizon decades ago. In 1961, he warned the American people in his farewell speech as president:

> Until the latest of our world conflicts, the United States had no armaments industry. American makers of plowshares could, with time and as required, make swords as well. But now we can no longer risk

emergency improvisation of national defense; we have been compelled to create a permanent armaments industry of vast proportions. . . . This conjunction of an immense military establishment and a large arms industry is new in the American experience. The total influence—economic, political, even spiritual—is felt in every city, every state house, every office of the federal government. We recognize the imperative need for this development. Yet we must not fail to comprehend its grave implications. Our toil, resources, and livelihood are all involved; so is the very structure of our society. In the councils of government, we must guard against the acquisition of unwarranted influence, whether sought or unsought, by the military industrial complex. The potential for the disastrous rise of misplaced power exists and will persist. We must never let the weight of this combination endanger our liberties or democratic processes. We should take nothing for granted. Only an alert and knowledgeable citizenry can compel the proper meshing of the huge industrial and military machinery of defense with our peaceful methods and goals, so that security and liberty may prosper together.

Ike knew we had made a deal with the devil. A permanent arms industry is a business motivated by profit, not moral sensibilities. War is a business opportunity.

Eisenhower's admonition that "only an alert and knowledgeable citizenry" can quell the problem worries me a great deal. I don't think Americans are trying hard enough to be informed. The brainwashing by the administration and right-wing media has been wildly successful. It has stifled debate. It has stifled freedom of speech.

If the American people continue to be stampeded like the nineteeth-century buffalo herds, our fate may mirror theirs. Francie Berg, a Hettinger, North Dakota, historian, writes, "By 1883, only 10,000 buffalo remained in the last herd. The end came in October 1883, when Sitting Bull and a thousand Sioux from Standing Rock [reservation] killed the last 1,100 buffalo about 15 to 20 miles southeast of what is now Hettinger."

The buffalo was nearly extinct.

Not all of them went down easy. Sometimes during a hunt, a wise old bull would figure it out. He would turn on his enemy. He would stop running and fight back.

There's No Defense for a War Without Debate

Ladies and gentlemen, I ask you, who is the defender of America's freedom? If your answer is the American soldier, or even the American media, that would be right. But who's really on the front line to protect the First Pillar? It's you, the American citizen.

When I reflect on the way my government and a jelly-legged mainstream press let America down in the wake of September 11, 2001, I cannot let the American people off the hook. We let ourselves down by failing to ask questions, by allowing ourselves to be led by the Pied Pipers of Propaganda on right-wing radio and television.

In many ways, President Bush reflects this nation's short attention span. Like too many Americans, he's disengaged and ill-informed. When debate was stifled, we didn't have the guts to speak up. When we were being told what we knew to be lies, we accepted them.

Apathy dooms us. I don't think we've shaken it off yet. More and more Americans feel disenfranchised. Our beliefs and opinions won't matter if we refuse to go to the polls. In the presidential election of 2000 only 51 percent of eligible voters voted. If you wanted

Al Gore to win but couldn't bear to pull yourself away from the television on election day, *you* are personally responsible for the state of affairs. In the mid-term congressional election of 1998, only 36 percent voted. In the June 2004 primary in my own state of North Dakota, which has no voter registration hurdle and historically shows strong voter turnout, a scant *19 percent* voted.

What the hell is that all about? Here we are with men and women fighting and dying in Iraq to create a democratic government, and at home we can't do better than 19 percent! I'm ashamed. What does that say about us as Americans? Plato said, "One of the penalties for refusing to participate in politics is that you end up being governed by your inferiors." In times like these, apathy kills.

I think back to the funeral of Jon Fettig, who was thirty years old when he died on July 22, 2003. He was the first North Dakota Army National Guard soldier killed in battle since the Korean War. Because Jon's death was the first in a small, close-knit state, the outpouring of support for the Fettig family was truly overwhelming. Jon's family wanted to use *The Ed Schultz Show* to say thank you. They also wanted people to know who Jon was—an All-American boy who loved his country and his life. *I* wanted North Dakota to know what it had lost.

You can tell a lot about a man by the grief his family feels when he is gone. Jon's young wife, Cody, was completely bewildered. She hugged me when the show was over. It was more than just a hug. She held me and held me, and would not let me go.

I wondered—I'm sure she did, too—if she would ever come to grips with her loss.

Most deeply etched in my memory is Jon's father, Larry, who was a veteran. I think this gave him a level of understanding that other fathers might not have had at such a loss, but this understanding did little to mitigate his grief. Larry confided that he had urged Jon to join the National Guard to pay for his college education. This must have weighed heavily on his conscience. He was incredibly proud of his son. Jon Fettig, who *loved* the military, was eager to serve in Iraq and couldn't stand the thought of his buddies from the 957th Engineer Company going off to war without him. In the end, he served and was awarded a Purple Heart and Bronze Star at his funeral.

The show was broadcast from Dickinson. It was a program filled with dramatic pauses. Sometimes silence is the only adequate expression of loss. It had a profound effect on Wendy and me. We mourned a man we would never know. Across North Dakota that day, many tears were shed for Jon Fettig. The boy next door was gone. I remember thinking about my own twenty-one-year-old son, Dave. I did what every father does, and imagined how it would feel if I lost him. It just about killed me. Now, whenever another soldier dies, I remember that he or she has a family like Jon Fettig's.

These are the things I think about when I recall the absence of debate during the feverish months leading up to the invasion of Iraq. Like so many Americans, I supported the president. I believed him. Now, I wonder why I didn't listen to that gut feeling I had that something wasn't right. I wonder why I didn't heed Senator Robert Byrd (D-VA) on February 12, 2003, five weeks before the war began, in a speech entitled, "We Stand Passively Mute." It may be one of the greatest speeches ever delivered on the Senate floor:

To contemplate war is to think about the most horrible of human experiences. On this February day, as this nation stands at the brink of battle, every American on some level must be contemplating the horrors of war. Yet, this Chamber is, for the most part, silent—ominously, dreadfully silent. There is no debate, no discussion, no attempt to lay out for the nation the pros and cons of this particular war. There is nothing.

We stand passively mute in the United States Senate, paralyzed by our own uncertainty, seemingly stunned by the sheer turmoil of events. Only on the editorial pages of our newspapers is there much substantive discussion of the prudence or imprudence of engaging in this particular war. And this is no small conflagration we contemplate. This is no simple attempt to defang a villain. No. This coming battle, if it materializes, represents a turning point in U.S. foreign policy and possibly a turning point in the recent history of the world.

This nation is about to embark upon the first test of a revolutionary doctrine applied in an extraordinary way at an unfortunate time. The doctrine of preemption—the idea that the United States or any other nation can legitimately attack a nation that is not imminently threatening but may be threatening in the future—is a radical new twist on the traditional idea of self-defense. It appears to be in contravention of international law and the U.N. Charter. And it is being tested at a time of worldwide terrorism, making many countries around the globe wonder if they will soon be on our—or some other nation's—hit list. . . .

There are huge cracks emerging in our time-honored alliances, and U.S. intentions are suddenly subject to damaging worldwide speculation. Anti-Americanism based on mistrust, misinformation, suspicion, and alarming rhetoric from U.S. leaders is fracturing the once solid alliance against global terrorism which existed after September 11.

Here at home, people are warned of imminent terrorist attacks with little guidance as to when or where such attacks might occur. Family members are being called to active military duty, with no idea of the duration of their stay or what horrors they may face. Communities are being left with less than adequate police and fire protection. Other essential services are also short-staffed. The mood of the nation is grim. The economy is stumbling. Fuel prices are rising and may soon spike higher. This Administration, now in power for a little over two years, must be judged on its record. I believe that that record is dismal. . . .

In foreign policy, this Administration has failed to find Osama bin Laden. In fact, just yesterday we heard from him again marshaling his forces and urging them to kill. This Administration has split traditional alliances, possibly crippling, for all time, international order-keeping entities like the United Nations and NATO. This Administration has called into question the traditional worldwide perception of the United States as well-intentioned peacekeeper. This Administration has turned the patient art of diplomacy into threats, labeling, and name calling of the sort that reflects quite poorly on the intelligence and sensitivity of our leaders, and which will have consequences for years to come.

Calling heads of state pygmies, labeling whole countries as evil, denigrating powerful European allies as irrelevant—these types of crude insensitivities can do our great nation no good. We may have massive military might, but we cannot fight a global war on terrorism alone. We need the cooperation and friendship of our time-honored allies as well as the newer found friends whom we can attract with our wealth. Our awesome military machine will do us little good if we suffer another devastating attack on our homeland which severely damages our economy. Our military manpower is already stretched thin and we will need the augmenting support of those nations who can supply troop strength, not just sign letters cheering us on . . .

And yet we hear little about the aftermath of war in Iraq. In the absence of plans, speculation abroad is rife. Will we seize Iraq's oil fields, becoming an occupying power which controls the price and supply of that nation's oil for the foreseeable future? To whom do we propose to hand the reins of power after Saddam Hussein?

Will our war inflame the Muslim world resulting in devastating attacks on Israel? Will Israel retaliate with its own nuclear arsenal? Will the Jordanian and Saudi Arabian governments be toppled by radicals, bolstered by Iran which has much closer ties to terrorism than Iraq?

. . . One can understand the anger and shock of any President after the savage attacks of September 11. One can appreciate the frustration of having only a shadow to chase and an amorphous, fleeting enemy on which it is nearly impossible to exact retribution.

But to turn one's frustration and anger into the kind of extremely destabilizing and dangerous foreign policy debacle that the world is currently witnessing is inexcusable from any Administration charged with the awesome power and responsibility of guiding the destiny of the greatest superpower on the planet. Frankly, many of the pronouncements made by this administration are outrageous. There is no other word.

Yet this chamber is hauntingly silent. On what is possibly the eve of horrific infliction of death and destruction on the population of the nation of Iraq—a population, I might add, of which over 50 percent is under age 15—this chamber is silent . . .

We are truly sleepwalking through history. In my heart of hearts I pray that this great nation and its good and trusting citizens are not in for a rudest of awakenings.

To engage in war is always to pick a wild card. And war must always be a last resort, not a first choice. I truly must question the judgment of any President who can say that a massive unprovoked military attack on a nation which is over 50 percent children is "in the highest moral traditions of our country." This war is not necessary at this time.

In one man's eloquent speech, the arguments against the war in Iraq were crystallized. But we weren't listening. What Byrd warned would happen has played out in the worst way.

By June 30, 2004, America had lost 859 soldiers in Iraq, with more than 5,000 wounded. The Iraq military lost an estimated 6,000. American casualties are well reported, but notice that we don't see many photographs of those flag-draped coffins. It's easier when the dead are just statistics. Lost in all of this is the fact that the Coalition of the Willing, with Don Rumsfeld's prized precision weapons, had killed an estimated 9,000 to 11,000 Iraqi civilians. Statistically, *half* of them must have been children. Figure 17,000 dead and rising. We don't have an exact number because our government decided simply to stop reporting civilian casualties. It's bad PR. By comparison, and in fairness to the estimated death toll, a *New York Times* article (January 27, 2003) estimated Saddam killed as many as 200,000 civilians in Iraq prisons since 1979.

America has been crippled militarily by the policies of the Bush administration. Do you think there was a reason Tommy Franks retired after the fall of Baghdad? I believe he got out because Don Rumsfeld would not listen to his protests about the relatively small size of the invasion force. It is evident that we had enough men to win the war, but not enough to stabilize the country. Franks wanted 250,000 soldiers, while Rumsfeld originally said 70,000 would be enough. In June 2004, America had about 138,000 soldiers in Iraq, not nearly enough to secure the infrastructure and oil pipelines.

General Anthony Zinni, former U.S. commander in the Middle East, says the Bush administration has put a huge strain on the military with the rush into Iraq. There has been unprecedented pressure put on the National Guard. Weekend warriors who should be at work shoring up our borders and protecting America's infrastructure are targets in Iraq, doing jobs for which they are not trained— as was so clearly illustrated at Abu Ghraib Prison. The public relations fallout from the torture of Iraqi prisoners was as real a defeat as any military setback. We came as liberators, right? We were there to win the hearts of the Iraqi people, weren't we?

Senator Joe Biden (D-DE) reminded John Ashcroft during a Senate Judiciary Committee hearing that America must abide by the Geneva Convention to "protect *my* son in the military. That's why we have these treaties. So when Americans are captured they are not tortured. That's the reason—in case anybody forgets it!"

What has happened in Iraq, absent the protections of the Geneva Convention, ought to give us pause before relinquishing our own constitutional freedoms through the Patriot Acts. A government that has the power over its people will eventually use it against them. Thomas Jefferson said, "Experience has shown that even under the best forms of government, those entrusted with power have, in time, and by slow operations, perverted it into tyranny."

American troops make up about 90 percent of the approximately 160,000 soldiers in Iraq (as of June 2004). In the first Gulf War, an estimated 200,000 soldiers from other countries joined a coalition force of 500,000 to drive Saddam out of Kuwait. In June 2004, the Coalition of the Willing had contributed about *15,000 troops.*

Of the approximately 138,000 army troops in Iraq in June 2004, *nearly half* were National Guard troops. There were about 20,000 troops in Afghanistan in the same time frame. To take some pressure off the troops in Iraq, the army reassigned 12,500 troops from South Korea—one-third of the 37,000 stationed there.

One of those soldiers, Pfc. David Baumann, a U.S. Army mechanic from Ashley, North Dakota, was startled to learn he would be on guard duty north of Baghdad. Though not yet twenty-one years old, Baumann understood that this was a historical deployment. "This is the first time in fifty years that troops are being deployed from Korea," he said. "No one has left [in the middle of a tour of duty] since the Korean War. We also aren't coming back here after the tour in Iraq." Just like that, a Humvee mechanic finds himself in a hot zone with a rifle instead of a wrench in his hands. Baumann, feeling invincible like all men of his age, is not concerned. His mother, Mary, a government conservation specialist, said, "All of a sudden they're not playing at war. . . . They *are* at war." In a country where most Americans have not been asked to sacrifice for the war effort, soldiers and their families are paying a steep price.

The *St. Louis Dispatch* tells the story of U.S. Marine Corps Staff Sgt. John Kelley, a veteran of Bosnia, Kosovo, and Somalia: "When U.S. forces moved into Iraq, his was among the first units to push into the country from Kuwait. Less than five months after his return to the United States, Kelley was back in Iraq, fighting insurgents just yards away from the Syrian border. That's when Kelley, an eleven-year veteran, learned through a Red Cross message that his oldest child, Kristen, ten, had put a knife to her throat and threatened to kill herself because she believed her father had been blown up. Kelley, thirty, immediately headed home from Iraq. But before he could get a flight out of Kuwait City to Germany and then to the United States, he received another note from the Red Cross. His mother, Susan Kelley, had been strangled, then beaten with a large tree limb and left for dead under a briar bush. She was in a coma in a Pittsburgh hospital and not expected to live." Kelley doesn't plan to reenlist because his absences have taken too large a toll on his family. "I'd like to stay," he said, "but it's killing the family."

The Army War College says the war has stretched our army in Iraq almost to its "breaking point." Clinton and Democrats are being blamed for gutting the military, but let's not forget that Dick Cheney, as Secretary of Defense under Reagan and Bush Senior, lobbied hard to reduce the military from 2.2 million to 1.6 million after winning the Cold War. Some people believe that the neocon go-it-alone policy will result in the demand for more soldiers. Recruitment has fallen. *Stars and Stripes* polling indicates almost half of the soldiers serving in Iraq won't reenlist.

Quietly, Selective Service has been gearing up to implement a draft within seventy-five days of the order. Bush won't tell you because it would kill any chance for reelection.

There is even legislation pending in Congress to renew the draft. Representative Charles Rangel (D-NY), who introduced the legislation, says it is primarily the poor and minorities serving in Iraq. Why? Because economic inequities deprive the poor of the same employment and education opportunities that more affluent Americans enjoy. Rangel says, "For those who say the poor fight better, I say give the rich a chance!"

For American servicemen and women, the draft has arrived. President George W. Bush has turned volunteers into conscripts by extending their tours in Iraq. In late June 2004, the army recalled to active duty some 5,000 men from Ready Reserve, some of whom had not worn a uniform or had military training for nearly eight years. "This was inevitable when it became clear that we would have to maintain significant combat forces in Iraq for a period of years," said military analyst Dan Goure in an *Associated Press* story.

Death is not the only form of war-time sacrifice. As observed in the *St. Louis Dispatch,* "The husbands and wives of some army reservists and National Guardsmen find themselves struggling to make ends meet because their spouses' military checks often are far below their civilian pay. Some small-business owners have been forced to sell off their firms. Others have watched their businesses go under."

Poor planning has turned the U.S. Army into a trap. It's not fair to the soldiers. It's not fair to their families back home. Now tell me again, who is supporting the troops? Here we are, on the eve of a possible draft—the first since 1973. Our borders are not properly defended. If we are defenseless at home, we appear clueless in Iraq. The administration planned only for a quick victory followed by dancing in the streets. There was no Plan B. I pray that we can work our way out of this mess. But it's ironic, isn't it? In the name of defending America, the Bush administration has left us more vulnerable than ever.

We Can't Back Down from Terrorism

Terrorism is the tool of the weak, but it can be an effective tool against America's First Pillar of defense if we allow it to dominate our psyches. Terrorists—and governments, for that matter—understand that fear, perhaps more than anything, can generate a predictable reaction from a population.

It's important to understand that while the threat against the nation is very real, the odds of any one American falling victim to terrorism are minute. These days, when I stand out on the vast prairie, I think, "It's gonna take a whole lot of terrorists to cover all *this* ground." In New York, where there are more people and more targets, my anxiety level would be higher. Still, only a sliver of our population is really at risk. I don't want to minimize it, but Americans must adapt a pragmatic approach to terrorism. High emotions play into the hands of the enemy. Americans must strive to understand the reasons we are under attack. While there is no rational justification for flying planes into buildings, we should think seriously about how America's foreign relations and policies have disaffected people in other countries.

We could learn something from American farmers, especially the old-timers. Many of them are missing fingers—a testament to the dangerous life on the farm. Many suffer hearing loss from long days riding tractors. Others develop skin cancer later in life. It's not uncommon to see an old-timer walking around with a band-aid on his face where a doctor has cut away the latest malignant cells to emerge. For some of these farmers, the cancer is nothing more than an inconvenience. They handle it with stoicism—either they get it or it gets them. Nothing seems to faze these prairie stoics. It's one of the traits I admire most about people from the heartland. In fact, I think stoicism is a tool we will need to implement in the battle against terrorism over the next several years.

Americans are still grappling with a way to deal with the atrocities that were once confined to the black and white lines of our newspapers. Since 9/11, Americans have had to process a lot of fear and heartache, as well as absorb a lot of new information. We've learned that virtually anything invented to serve mankind can also be used to attack mankind. The Internet, which has been appropriated as a psychological tool of terror, has served up pictures of innocent beheaded Americans. I wish I could offer more than stoicism as a protective device, but that's all I've got. For years, we've watched Israel deal with bombings on almost a daily basis. Now, it seems, their world is becoming ours.

If the core of my First Pillar of Defense is homeland security, another key ingredient is understanding. Americans have a short attention span. Many other cultures take a long view of history. They see us in a different light than we see ourselves. To really understand the phenomenon of terrorism, we have to try to understand their perspective.

Americans have been under the shadow of modern terrorism since 1979 when Iranian students grabbed fifty-two Americans and held them for 444 days, demanding that our nation turn over the deposed Shah of Iran, who was dying of cancer in America.

1979 was a pivotal year in history, though who could know that then? It marked the beginning of Osama bin Laden's emergence as an opponent to the Soviet Union's invasion of Afghanistan. Bin Laden, then a twenty-three-year-old Saudi engineering graduate, left his family's construction business to help the Mujahideen rebellion against the USSR. After his election in 1980, Reagan supported the Mujahideen as part of the Cold War fight against the Soviets. It's interesting to note the willingness of the U.S. government to support Muslim extremists when we were not the target.

In 1979, Saddam Hussein became leader of Iraq. By 1980, Iraq and Iran were engaged in a bloody eight-year war in which the U.S. allied with Saddam. Imagine, only a quarter century ago, the United States was aligned with both Saddam *and* Osama bin Laden.

We had become enemies of Iran after the overthrow of the Shah, a man the CIA (under Eisenhower) helped put in power in 1953 after toppling Prime Minister Mossadegh. Mossadegh's sin was planning to nationalize the country's oil industry, to the detriment of Western oil companies. That was the first in a long list of post-World War II CIA interventions. The United States lost a valuable ally in the Middle East, leaving Saudi Arabia as the only major oil producer with which the United States had close ties. In Saudi Arabia, we support a monarchy that could not exist without our protection and influence. And yet, we keep hearing that oil has nothing to do with the U.S. interest in the Middle East. The region contains *more than half* of the world's known oil reserves. America gets about 30 percent of its oil from the Middle East. We'd be fools *not* to be interested.

Secretary of State Madeleine Albright once commented on U.S. meddling in Iran: "The Eisenhower administration believed its actions were justified for strategic reasons. But the coup was clearly a setback for Iran's political development and it is easy to see now why many Iranians continue to resent this intervention by America."

By 1985, Reagan and *Fox News* star Ollie North began selling arms to Iran in exchange for hostages, diverting money from the sale to the Contras in Nicaragua, a group created by the CIA, who were fighting the *elected* Marxist Sandinista government.

Americans are only now beginning to understand how the world perceives us. We are viewed much as Germany was in 1938 when it started World War II. Do I think that's fair? I think we're better than that. But unless WMDs are found in Iraq, and even if the Iraqis end up better off under a moderate government, the world will consider the war unjustified. America is viewed as an imperialist country because we *have* been imperialistic. President Bush's simplistic argument that we're under attack because "[the terrorists] hate freedom," is nonsense. It just doesn't wash. If they hated freedom, they would handcuff themselves to the bed and that would be that. Terrorism is more complicated than that.

In the 1820s, President James Monroe declared in the Monroe Doctrine that European powers must stay out of North and South American countries. The doctrine also proclaimed that the United States had the right to intervene *anywhere* in the hemisphere to ensure its security. This was the pretext for the Reagan Doctrine, which supported anti-Communist forces in Central America.

Later in the nineteenth century and into the early years of the twentieth century, presidents McKinley, Theodore Roosevelt, and Taft adopted a policy that the United States must broaden its influence across the globe in order to serve "American interests." They believed it was our country's duty to spread democracy. So America opened branch offices in other countries, including the Philippines and Cuba.

Woodrow Wilson viewed it differently. He said America should intervene to *defend* democracies, not promote them. Yet, despite his

World War I isolationism, and in contrast to his stated principles, he intervened in Nicaragua, Haiti, and the Dominican Republic, and fought a war with Mexico.

It wasn't until after World War II that America really stepped up its covert actions, beginning with Eisenhower's foray into Iran. We champion democracy, but we embrace dictators when it suits our needs. How can other nations possibly know what to make of America's schizophrenic diplomacy? We helped overthrow elected governments. We had armed Iran *and* Iraq. The war between them is estimated to have killed well over a million people.

It devastated both countries economically and paved the way for the first Gulf War. After the war, Saddam quarreled with Kuwait over money that Iraq borrowed during the war with Iran. He also accused Kuwait of exceeding OPEC oil production limits (thereby driving down prices) and stealing oil from Iraqi oil fields on the border between the two countries by using horizontal drilling.

Despite the escalation of the feud, on July 25, 1990, U.S. Ambassador April Glaspie told Hussein that America has "no opinion on the Arab-Arab conflicts, like your border disagreement with Kuwait." We might as well have issued an invitation. About a week after the U.S. ambassador gave Saddam the green light, Iraq invaded Kuwait.

Was it bad diplomacy on our part, or a trap?

The borders of the Middle East were originally drawn by Britain and France after World War I. They divided up conquered Turkish territory, creating puppet states. France claimed Lebanon and Syria. Britain got Palestine, Jordan, and Iraq, where they installed King Faisal. When oil was discovered in Iraq, America, by then an emerging world power, got into the action, helping force a settlement that divided Iraqi oil between Britain, France, Holland, and the United States. The Iraqi people got virtually nothing.

Resentful of oil wealth profits going to foreign companies, the Iraqis staged a coup in 1958. In response, Eisenhower sent 20,000

Marines to Lebanon, poised to invade Iraq under the tenants of the Eisenhower Doctrine that said the United States would intervene directly to protect its interests in the Middle East. Chinese and Soviet support of the new Iraqi government forced Eisenhower to back down. Still, the United States continued to support Kurdish insurgents in northern Iraq.

That brings us to the ethnic make-up of Iraq. The current Iraq War leaves us with a complicated balance of the *Kurds* in the north, the *Sunni* minority, and the *Shia* majority.

The Kurds, who were gassed by Saddam while Bush Senior looked the other way, are also oppressed in Turkey, an American ally. The Kurds, with Iraq's largest militia of 75,000, will have a hard time supporting any government designed by Americans. We have sold them down the river before.

American diplomacy has been *consistently inconsistent* in the region. We have helped stir up hornet nests over the years, and now we are being stung by terrorism. What do bin Laden and other Islamic extremists want? They want us out. Bin Laden wants us out of Saudi Arabia (and the Middle East) so a strict Muslim Wahhabi-style government can be established. Religious extremism is the root of his plan.

So how do we approach this problem? If we simply pull out, we doom these countries to severe repression. As a nation, America must learn to take the long view of its global actions. With our short attention spans, we like quick fixes. That has not and will not work in the Middle East—or anywhere, for that matter. It doesn't help that we have presidents who are more interested in getting reelected than in implementing long-term political solutions. America, as a country, must develop a coherent, *long range,* pragmatic, and just approach to world affairs.

I agree with President Bush's plan to take the fight to al Qaeda. However, we must proceed much more pragmatically against state sponsors of terrorism. Just because diplomacy with al Qaeda is not an option, doesn't mean we shouldn't pursue it elsewhere. Libya has shown signs of abandoning its terrorist ways. While that may well be a result of the Iraq invasion, I think the Iraq War has distracted us from the more crucial issue of defeating al Qaeda. Americans are justified in questioning our involvement in Iraq, but we must be of one mind when it comes to the pursuit of al Qaeda. We must prove over time that we will not back down, that we're in this for the long haul.

In the past, we have given terrorists the impression that we are unwilling to stick it out when things get tough. Some hold Vietnam as an example. Others point to a series of inconsistent reactions to terrorism under Republican and Democratic administrations. These arguments have merit. All the more reason, then, to take a long measured look at the wisdom of entering any war—be it Iraq or Vietnam. Americans must be convinced it is a just cause. We will not fight a war we do not believe in.

Curiously, the State Department global terrorism report issued in April 2004 said that terrorist attacks were *down* in 2003 to a record low since 1969. But it is clear that terrorism is on the rise. Representative Henry Waxman (D-CA) charged the Bush administration with manipulating figures to show a drop in terrorism for political gain. Secretary of State Colin Powell, the administration's designated apologizer, called the report "a mistake." Apparently the administration's inability to add and subtract in the budgeting process has carried over to the war on terror.

Did the spark we ignited in Iraq play a part in the worldwide increase of terrorism? I think so. I think we played into bin Laden's grand plan to inflame Muslims against America. We had the sympathy of the world when we declared war on bin Laden and the Taliban. Virulent Muslim anti-American sentiments did not escalate until we threatened Iraq. We made bin Laden's case for him. From the perspective of Muslims in the Middle East, who have long suffered at the hands of U.S. interventions, the Yankee Imperialists were back at it again. The Iraq invasion has helped terrorists bring in new recruits.

A real key is bin Laden's home, Saudi Arabia, where America has supported a repressive regime to secure the Saudi oil supply. The main goal is to drive the infidels (that's us) from Muslim territory in Saudi Arabia and Iraq. Bin Laden announced, "To America, I say only a few words to it and its people. I swear by God, who has elevated the skies without pillars, neither America nor the people who live in it will dream of security before we live it in Palestine, and not before all the infidel armies leave the land of Mohammed, peace be upon him."

Most Muslims don't want a repressive religious regime like the one bin Laden envisions. But when we bomb the hell out of them, as we did in Iraq, we force them in that direction. And as long as we're camped in Muslim territories, Islamic terrorism will be with us. Bin Laden stopped attacking Russia when they withdrew from Afghanistan. Of course, they are still dealing with Islamic terrorism in Chechnya. There are no guarantees. Some believe al Qaeda's larger goal is a holy war between Islam and Christianity.

Iraqis won't accept long-term occupation by American troops. Yet, if we leave too early, we risk leaving the situation far more unstable than it was when we first got there. If a Muslim extremist government emerges, we will have taken one giant step backward. Catch 22. The best option is to stick it out, although we're going to lose a lot of soldiers and we won't see help from our allies until Americans elect a president other world leaders trust. Ultimately, if we insist on a presence in the Middle East, we have to do so in a manner that wins the hearts of the Muslim populace, thereby eroding support for bin Laden and other terrorist networks. We have to wear white hats again.

Alan Dershowitz, in his book *Why Terrorism Works,* differentiates between the "apocalyptic terrorism" of al Qaeda and the "rational terrorism" of groups like the Palestinian Liberation Organization (PLO). Neither kind of terrorism, he says, is caused by frustration, disenfranchisement, or poverty. I don't know if I completely agree with him, but he makes an interesting argument. Dershowitz also says that, in the case of the PLO, terrorism has worked. They've garnered the sympathy of other nations. Yasser Arafat has won a Nobel Peace Prize and made numerous visits to the Clinton White House. They have moved their agenda forward. But Dershowitz warns against ever giving in to terrorists. If you negotiate to release hostages, he says, you doom others to be taken hostage.

To ease tensions in the Middle East, I believe we must follow through with the creation of a Palestinian homeland. I do not believe peace can be achieved without it. In that case, will terrorism have succeeded? Arguably, yes. Terrorism seemed to work when on March 14, 2004, following the al Qaeda train bombings in Madrid, the Spanish elected a Socialist "peace candidate," Jose Luis Rodriguez Zapatero, as prime minister. He denounced the U.S. invasion of Iraq and ensured noncooperation from Spain.

We are certain to see more terrorist attacks on American soil. That is the hard truth in all of this. I was at a briefing in 2004, when Clinton's former Secretary of Defense William Perry said there is a "better than even chance" that America will be hit by a dirty bomb within the next five years. It's a sobering thought. More ominous is the Bush administration's willingness to manipulate public fear for its own ends. As this book was in its final stages, the administration floated the idea of postponing the election. I told my listeners that, while the president could declare martial law, only Congress could postpone an election. Bush, however, was seeking the power to have one of his appointees make that decision. One of my callers observed that this would essentially be a coup.

Al Gore said in unrelated speech:

I am convinced that our founders would counsel us today that the greatest challenge facing our republic is not terrorism, as serious a threat as that is, but how we react to terrorism; and not war, but how we manage our fears and achieve security without losing our freedom. I am also convinced that they would warn us that democracy itself is in grave danger if we allow any president to use his role as commander in chief to rupture the careful balance between the executive, legislative and judicial branches of government. Our current president has gone to war and declared that our nation is now in a permanent state of war, which he says justifies his reinterpretation of the Constitution in ways that increase his personal power as president at the expense of Congress, the courts, and every individual citizen. We must surrender some of our traditional American freedoms, he tells us, so that he may have sufficient power to protect us against those who would do us harm.

Ask yourself, are we safer than we were before the Soviet Union fell? Yes, we are. There were thousands of nuclear missiles pointed across the ocean. But now we have terrorism and huge border security issues. We will not soon extricate ourselves from our dangerous global entanglements. This generation will continue to be put to the test. We must be resolute. We must make good decisions and then follow through.

When you connect the dots between America's crucial oil interests in the Middle East, it becomes obvious to me that the sooner America can establish energy independence with efficient use of wind, solar, fuel cell, and even clean-burning coal technologies, the sooner we can extricate ourselves from the tangled web of Middle East intrigue and war.

DEFENDING AMERICA SOLUTIONS

- *Border security:* First, we have to fund homeland security. Paramount is border security, with particular attention to our ports. We must inspect shipping containers. Also, proposed cuts to emergency personnel must be restored.

- *Intelligence:* "We in Congress would not have authorized that war . . . if we knew what we know now," said Senator Rockefeller (D-WV), vice chairman of the Senate Select Committee on Intelligence, in a July 9, 2004, *United Press International* report. Senator Ron Wyden (D-OR) said, "It is clear that the administration compounded the failures of the intelligence community by exaggerating and manipulating the community's conclusions to the public."

  With George Tenet's resignation, there's an opportunity to reorganize and reprioritize the CIA with close congressional oversight. It's important that communications between the FBI and CIA on down to local law enforcement improve. Most importantly, the CIA's covert actions must be more closely monitored—again by congressional oversight.

  The 9/11 Commission's recommendation for a national intelligence director is a good one. However, a position like this consolidates an extreme amount of power and must be put into place with enough checks and balances. Other 9/11 Commission plans to secure our borders, inspect cargo, and increase rail and other modes of transportation must be implemented. We must do so in a manner that does not overtly infringe on American liberty and with the tacit understanding that any free society such as ours will always be vulnerable. We must expand the pool of human resources—spies, if you will. When Bush made the decision to invade Iraq, Arabic-speaking soldiers and intelligence resources had to be pulled from Afghanistan to Iraq.

- *Accountability:* While the 9/11 Commission has examined security breakdowns, the administration must be held accountable on several other fronts. To reestablish global credibility, the Abu Ghraib prison investigation must be public and transparent. The president must come clean on his connections to the bin Ladens and other Saudis. There must be an ethics commission formed to investigate the direct connections between government contractors and members of the administration. Also, Reagan's presidential papers must be released so Americans can learn who President Bush is trying to protect. We must demand a true accounting of the cost of the war in dollars and in casualties— specifically, civilian casualties. We know the price American soldiers are paying. We must also know the price Iraqi civilians are paying.

- *Regaining the trust of the military:* The treatment of the American soldier by this administration is an outrage. Poor planning has led to extended tours of duty and overuse of the National Guard. Calling up inactive servicemen for a war that did not need to be fought has sent a message to possible recruits that the military could be a trap. Worse yet, we are on the brink of a draft. We are much better served if a soldier wants to be there. Cutting pay and benefits is an insult. Veterans must receive the best health care. Our Veterans Administration must be properly funded, and the commitments we have made to our soldiers honored. Their commitment to America has far exceeded our commitment to them. I agree with Rumsfeld's theory of a fast, fluid military. We have a military designed to fight other armies. An overwhelming force is fine for invading and occupying a country. Battling terrorism requires swifter, smaller forces. We need to be able to do both.

- *Energy policy:* First we need to hear from Dick Cheney what policies were discussed in the secret energy meetings. Americans need to demand and embrace new technologies to ease our dependence on foreign oil. Buy that electric car. Conserve energy. If you have to drive through snow banks every winter, an SUV makes sense. But do you need a Hummer in Burbank? This SUV thing is out of hand. (Under the Clinton administration, emissions rose 14 percent!) Our government needs to aggressively fund wind technology. Subsidize? You bet. In essence, all our troops in Iraq are subsidizing our gasoline by ensuring a safe supply from the Middle East.

  Fuel cell technology is on the horizon. Bio fuels make economic sense. The late Dwight Baumann, a former North Dakotan who taught engineering design at Carnegie Mellon University in Pittsburgh, converted his 1984 Volvo to run on vegetable oil. The car gets the same gas mileage from vegetable oil as it does on regular diesel fuel. It's cheaper, too—about a dollar a gallon. This is nothing new to farmers. I've heard of old tractors that ran on used oil. More ethanol production would give an economic boost to farmers and help ease our dependence on oil.

- *Global strategy:* We must carefully assess the Bush Doctrine of preemptive strikes. If other nations adopt such a policy, we have, in a sense, legitimized war at any time for any reason. We must rebuild our relationships with other countries, and we must work harder within the confines of the United Nations. There can be no credible United Nations if the United States does not behave responsibly. To undermine support for Islamic terrorists, America must look for ways to improve relationships with Muslim populations. Economic sanctions breed discontent. Past and present support of dictatorships in Iran, Iraq, Saudi Arabia, and Pakistan created misery for citizens of those countries. We must give more than lip service to human rights.

THE SECOND PILLAR

A SOUND ECONOMY

THE PROBLEM

We are seeing an historic concentration of wealth among a very small percentage of Americans—globally, too. This includes people in government—and those well-connected to the government—who make policies, like the $1.6 trillion tax cut for the wealthy. While capitalism remains the best machine to fuel a civilization, such a severe imbalance in wealth is a danger; that's why most other industrialized countries aren't afraid to tax the rich and provide more social programs for the poor and middle class. In these largely peaceful countries, health care is a right, not a privilege. In our country, corrupt alliances between big business and government have created a stranglehold on power. This unholy alliance has left the common man unprotected, as outsourced jobs continue to kill middle American families.

How does this affect me? Well, if you're rich, you can relax—at least until the peasants are at the gate with pitchforks and burning torches. If you're a middle-class American, on the other hand, you'll continue to pay a larger percentage of your wages in taxes than many businesses and wealthy Americans. You are also funding a tax break legislated by the rich for the rich. Where's the money coming from? Social Security. This administration has taken money from the poor and middle class to give to the wealthy. And now they say your Social Security payments might have to be cut back. I suspect the hidden agenda of the neocons is to eliminate social programs completely. Huge corporations like Enron have run amok, trashing 401k accounts and rattling Wall Street. In the process, they also managed to price-fix the supply of energy in this country, and you paid for it with higher electric bills. Our government—and it isn't just this administration—has not slowed the outsourcing of jobs. Companies have been *rewarded* for shipping jobs like yours overseas. If you're unemployed, how can you afford your pitchfork and torch?

Corruption Is Killing the Middle Class and the Economy

In America, our Second Pillar—the economy—is approaching a breaking point. Who's most vulnerable? The heavily indebted middle class and poor. Never underestimate the role money plays in your life—even if you don't have any. You are governed by the rich, whose elections are financed by the rich, so that the elected rich can return the favors to their rich friends. It sounds incredibly cynical, but when you look at the evidence, how can you come to any other conclusion?

I'm not here to depress you, and I'm not here to tell you to give up. I'm here to give it to you straight. I've got faith that when the majority of Americans grasp what's going on around them, they'll start acting like a bear fresh out of hibernation—famished, ill-tempered, and ready to start raising hell.

It'll make the Reagan Revolution look like a Sunday school picnic. Forget about winning one for the Gipper—America needs to win one for Joe Six Pack! We're starved for a victory over the ruling elite. We need a populist Congress and a populist president who can work both sides of the aisle.

The president is a baseball man. What any baseball man knows is that when your pitcher has lost his stuff, you send in a new pitcher. And I gotta tell you, folks, Bush is throwing screwballs into the dirt. As an American, you're the manager. You get to decide if we make a change. And the change starts now.

Here's one way to do it: If you're really ambitious, run for office yourself.

Before I was offered my national show, I was as serious as a heart attack about seeking the Democratic nomination to run against North Dakota's incumbent governor, John Hoeven—not because I want to be a politician, but because Hoeven is so inept. I knew I could do better. I *wanted* to do better. That's the difference between us. John Hoeven is a spoiled rich kid whose daddy's money got him elected to a job he doesn't care about. That job is about fighting for the little guy. But Hoeven is *indifferent* to the little guy. He wanted the governor's office as a trophy entry on his resume. And because we the people didn't stand up to stop him, Hoeven got elected, and proved one of the sad facts about politics in America today: A few million dollars can buy you a governor's office.

I don't know if I could have mustered the financial backing to beat Hoeven, but I would have cleaned his clock in every debate. Around the same time I was thinking about running, though, I was offered the chance to do a national radio show. "You can do more for North Dakota with the national program," my friends told me, and that helped me make up my mind.

It's my job to do what baseball umpires do: Call 'em like I see 'em. Every administration has its weaknesses. But when historians measure the unethical and illegal actions of the Bush administration, Bill

Clinton will come off looking like a Boy Scout. For every scumbag in government, there's another one on the outside. After all, there are only so many elected positions; why bother getting elected when you can just buy the votes you need? Californians will remember George Bush's buddy, "Kenny Boy" Lay, and the 2001 energy crisis perpetuated by Lay's company, Enron. Lay's dreams of becoming energy secretary have vanished under the shadow of indictments for his alleged role in robbing shareholders by cooking the books to present a more attractive balance sheet. And for wiping out Enron employees' 401k accounts, many of which were heavily weighted with Enron stock—stock that became worthless after the malfeasance was reported.

California's energy crisis, which Enron labored so hard to produce, cost the state an estimated $45 billion over two years. Not only did the state with the world's sixth largest economy pay higher electricity costs than the rest of the nation, its citizens and businesses lost business due to blackouts and a slowdown in economic growth, according to a study on the crisis.

We know now the whole thing was a sham. Enron orchestrated the crisis and manufactured the shortage for profit, pure and simple, by sending energy out of state to create the shortage in California. Tape recordings of company executives revealed just how conscious these jokers were about what they were doing. "What we need to do is to help in the cause of, ah, downfall of California," one of them said, in tape recordings obtained by CBS News. "You guys need to pull your megawatts out of California on a daily basis."

And here's my favorite: "You gotta think the economy is going to fucking get crushed, man. This is like a recession waiting to fucking happen."

There you have it. If there was ever a time for Teddy Roosevelt to leap out of the grave and start kicking corporate tails, this is it. We don't need more deregulation. These people abuse every bit of power they have. We need a crackdown of epic proportions. This isn't shady business. It's criminal.

Ken Lay is your president's *friend*? Holy smokes, I'm surprised you can't find his face in a deck of cards! Think about it. These people didn't care about the reverberations their schemes would send through the economy. They *gloried* in the idea that they could start a recession. Well, congratulations, boys. You did it. When huge companies like *Enron* fold, it rattles Wall Street, and innocent investors—who don't have the privilege of insider trading—get hurt.

Now, ask yourself what kind of energy policy Dick Cheney was hatching in the early months of the Bush II presidency, and why he fought all the way to the Supreme Court to keep those meeting records secret. Cheney admits that Kenny Boy was there. Can't you picture them poring over the maps of Iraq's oil fields? It astonishes me that Cheney's duck-hunting buddy, Supreme Court Justice Antonin Scalia, refused to recuse himself, despite the obvious conflict of interest.

But we're not trying to hide anything, they insist. *Oh, no.* What? Do they think we all just fell off a turnip truck? The issue is pretty simple. Follow me, now: Our elected vice president was in those meetings to plan energy strategy for the people of the United States—but he can't *tell* the people of the United States exactly what kind of energy policy they were discussing. Why—because it's just *so* good, he'd be smothered in kisses by a grateful nation?

Look around you. Check the prices at the gas pump. If they manipulated electricity in California, do you have any doubt they're manipulating gas prices? Do you think that when big companies have you by the balls, they're not going to squeeze? To paraphrase Forrest Gump, *Rotten is as rotten does.*

And what about the annual spike in heating fuel prices? That's all brought on by demand, right? Well, that's what they *want* us to think. At this point, I don't trust any big energy company—except to gouge you for every penny you have. And then, they'll rifle through the pockets of your frozen grandmother's corpse to make sure they got it all.

Nothing will change unless you demand it. All of this affects you—even if you *haven't* been getting sky-high electric bills, or you haven't yet lost your job or seen your Enron 401k go in the toilet. Enron, WorldCom, Tyco—every one of those outfits did you irreparable harm. The recession they helped create and prolong affected you. If you have a 401k, the wobbly stock market cost you. It cost plenty of people their jobs; for even the lucky ones, it cost them potential raise. And the bad economy helped drive up the national debt that you and your children will have to pay. *Seven trillion,* baby.

Ruthless companies like these set the stage for recession. September 11 took us the rest of the way down. They wonder why investor enthusiasm is down. Because we can't trust the prospectus! We need Ashcroft to stop spying on the librarians of America, and start focusing on the criminals again. And I'm not talking about Martha Stewart. We need the Securities and Exchange Commission and Federal Trade Commission to grow some fangs, and start going after the big guns.

If Americans don't beat back the corporate hucksters and neocon apologists, the middle class will continue to erode until there's nothing left. The American worker is the bedrock of this country, and conservatives have lost sight of that.

Even bedrock can be broken down. Mount Rushmore, the famous granite carving in our sister state of *South* Dakota (even national reporters get that wrong), requires regular attention to combat the effects of erosion. Water settles into cracks and freezes, widening cracks. Without constant maintenance, eventually George Washington's nose would fall off.

The Second Pillar—a sound economy—must include a vibrant middle class. If an economy doesn't benefit the majority, that's a big problem. There's a cold wet wind blowing through this country today, blowing good American jobs offshore and replacing them with low-paying service industry jobs. *Oh, but what wonderful prices we're seeing from those low-paid Chinese workers without health care.* Yeah, it's great. But if everyone in America is working for minimum wage, who's gonna buy the stuff? Henry Ford understood this better one hundred years ago than we do today: He knew that if he paid his workers enough, they could afford to buy his cars. But nobody in the White House today understands as much about such basic principles as old Hank did. Each month we set a new record trade deficit. We have a $46 billion trade imbalance *a month!* I know I'm just a talk show host, but I'm fairly certain you can't build a national economy on consumers alone.

American companies are sending plenty of jobs overseas, though, and they're almost giddy about it. Consider this, from the June 1, 2003, *CIO Magazine,* which targets large company executives as its readers: "Today, Indian outsourcing is one of the best ways for CIOs to cut application development and maintenance costs, deal effectively with the peaks and valleys of software demands, and focus on more strategic work. Depending on whom you ask, *anywhere from one-half to two-thirds of all Fortune 500 companies are already outsourcing to India,* and, according to Forrester Research, the amount of work done there for U.S. companies is expected to more than double this year. If you're not already sending some development or maintenance work to Mumbai or Chennai, chances are you're either looking into it or your CFO, salivating over potential labor cost savings of 70 percent, is wondering why you aren't."

But let's look at the other side of that problem. One of the hardest stories I had to tell on *The Ed Schultz Show* was in January 2004, when Electrolux AB, a refrigerator manufacturer that's been operating in Greenville, Michigan, since the late 1890s, closed its doors, putting 2,700 people out of work in a town of eight thousand. Why? Because they weren't making money? No. Because they weren't making *enough* money. The company, which makes the Frigidaire and Kenmore brands, moved the plant to Mexico.

Faced with the death knell of an entire city, a task force rallied and offered tax incentives worth $43 million a year to the company. The union pitched in, offering concessions of $32 million annually. It wasn't enough. The city will lose 20 percent of its tax base, killing the infrastructure of the community. The task force has been forced to turn its energies to a new task: helping the unemployed.

"Outside the factory," wrote one Associated Press reporter, "Greenville resident Gene Beckler sat in his parked pickup truck, waiting for a chance to comfort some of his friends and former colleagues when they emerged. 'I watched this whole plant grow,' said Beckler, who retired from Electrolux five years ago after spending thirty-three years as a press operator at the sprawling complex. 'It was just a little bitty plant when I first got here.'"

Many of these workers gave their lives to this company—and the company made money! The only thing that Electrolux lacked was *loyalty*—not worker loyalty, but corporate loyalty. These loyal workers deserved better: After all, they made the company successful. "We're always willing to work with an employer to preserve jobs," said Don Oetman of United Auto Workers Local 137, the union representing the workers. "But we're not willing to engage in a race to the bottom and trade away the wages, health care, and retirement security that make our members' jobs worth having in the first place."

Stories like these are hitting small towns across America. But at long last there are a few leaders who seem to be waking to the problem. Michigan Senator Debbie Stabenow has taken the issue to

Congress. She's co-sponsoring legislation to give tax incentives to companies to keep jobs in America.

Outsourcing is one more insidious way to erode unions. And let me tell you, when there are no unions protecting the American worker, how do you think corporate America is going to treat its workers? About as well as Enron treated California. According to final 2003 labor statistics, U.S. union workers were paid an average of $20.56 an hour—compared to $16.00 for nonunion workers. But the big difference between average union and nonunion workers plays out in benefits: When you include health insurance and retirement plans, union compensation is $31.82, compared to $21.85 for nonunion workers.

Big corporations don't like unions because they protect American workers. Joe Union isn't getting rich—he's making a little less than $43,000 before taxes. As any businessman knows—and *I* know, as an operations manager of my radio station—payroll is the biggest expense in the budget for virtually all businesses. So in the relentless rush to the bottom line, what do large corporations do? They send good jobs overseas, and fire the same American workers who helped build the country.

It used to be that there was a reliable bond of loyalty between a company and its workers. But that's increasingly looking like a thing of the past. When American workers lose good paying jobs, as they have under Bush—2.9 million—they can pretty much count on having to accept a lower wage, if they're lucky enough to return to the workforce at all.

John Kerry has been accused of negative thinking for calling Bush's record on job loss the worst since the Great Depression. Sorry, folks, that's not political spin—*it's a fact.* Facts are neither negative or positive. We've had two Bushes in office, and both of their administrations have largely been mired in recession. Maybe it's just bad luck.

But boy, those Bush boys sure know how to spank Saddam's sorry ass. It's a good thing they captured him alive. When Jeb Bush is presiding over the third Bush administration years from now (don't think he isn't planning it), and he finds himself staring at a third Bush recession, maybe he can trot Saddam out of his cell—hell, out of the grave—and declare him an imminent threat. At least when we invade San Quentin, it won't cost as much. (Halliburton is sure to get a no-bid contract to rebuild the prison.)

We're becoming a low-wage country. The drain of good-paying American jobs is truly eroding the bedrock of our society. The middle class pays the taxes, fights the wars, and provides a moral compass for the nation. But we're fast becoming a nation of haves and have-nots. You've seen the statistics on the alarming concentration of wealth in the hands of just a few Americans. Bill Gates owns more wealth than the bottom 45 percent of American households combined. In 1999, he was worth $81.5 *billion*. These days, he's been edged out for the top spot by one of the Walton Gang.

All of this worries me a great deal. But I want to make it clear that I'm not advocating class warfare. Every good job I ever had was working for a rich man. Mr. Gates, I don't mind the big paycheck, but could you at least give me a computer that works? Anytime *any* company dominates its industry like Microsoft does, there's little motivation for the company to improve and give the public cheaper and better products.

But with the balance becoming more and more extreme, with middle-class America actually sliding backward economically, we're setting the stage for the collapse of the system. It's in the news constantly—American workers are losing ground. Why? Because of scenarios like the one with Electrolux in Greenville, Michigan. A nation comprised of McWorkers and the unemployed will kill the economy, and the big corporations who've pulled the plug on the tornadic flush of jobs overseas will follow them right down the drain. The middle class drives the economy. Always has, always will. If Mom and Pop don't have disposable income, the businesses of America will fold like an Abu Graib detainee with electrodes in his pants.

It won't happen overnight, but make no mistake—it's happening. When do we hit the point of no return? No one really knows. I know we need to reward American companies for employing Americans and penalize with taxes and tariffs those who send jobs overseas. Yes, we are in a global economy. The natural order of things will cause jobs and products to flow more freely across borders. But consider that America is the financial engine that drives the world economy. If she falters, the world economy will be dragged down, too.

Our economy must be protected above all others. We must manage our place in the world market more carefully. We must work for long-term stability, even if it means the occasional loss of a few percentage points of short-term profit. We should insist on a world minimum wage, which would serve the dual purpose of lifting the standard of living for workers in third-world countries while allowing American products to be more competitive. It would slow the flow of jobs out of America. Perhaps foreign workers would start buying products from America! At least they'd be able to afford the DVD players they're assembling.

In recessions and depressions, the wealthy in all countries always emerge virtually unscathed. CEOs, who make obscene salaries, just don't care.

The Bush administration loves to talk about patriotism. Let me ask you, mister, how patriotic is it to send good jobs to communist China, while Joe Six Pack waits on the unemployment line? This administration has given the job exodus the green light. As long as they have their campaign contributions, they're fine.

The Bush administration has intentionally weakened the worker base. With Bush and his Republican Congress in the process of callously eliminating some overtime pay for eight million workers, it's clear they couldn't care less about what might benefit the American worker? *I know* limiting overtime helps big business. But for many American workers, that overtime check makes the difference between paying the mortgage or not. For a significant portion of the American workforce, it can amount to nearly half of their paycheck. Worker productivity continues to rise year by year, yet paychecks don't reflect that.

I'll say it again: Just because a business is big doesn't mean it is evil. But we must always watch large corporations closely, because they have the potential to do great harm. Business and government have become one and the same. Today, unfortunately, the fox is guarding the henhouse in Washington. These guys want to privatize everything. They want you to believe you'll save money—I doubt it—and in the long run, we leave ourselves financially vulnerable to untrustworthy corporations who are more worried about their bottom line than yours.

When you examine co-President Cheney's connections to Halliburton—the company to which he gave a free pass into Iraq so it could overcharge the American taxpayer $61 million for gasoline—and you try to make sense of the continuing flow of information about his actions while at the helm of Halliburton, you have to wonder. When Cheney complained on the Senate floor about Vermont Democratic Senator Patrick Leahy's inquiries into questionable Halliburton dealings in Iraq, Cheney told Leahy to "go fuck himself"—which may be an indirect violation of the don't ask-don't tell policy.

The economy—our Second Pillar—is wobbly . . . very wobbly indeed.

The Wal-Mart Effect

There's a silent crisis growing in America. America's plunge into the global economy is draining America of good-paying manufacturing jobs, while leaving poor-paying service industry jobs behind. We are experiencing the Wal-Martization of America.

In the race to the bottom line, big business may be winning— but the working man is still waiting for the starting gates to open.

According to 2004 figures, there are eight million unemployed American workers. That number may be closer to 14 million, after you factor in the people who have given up looking for jobs, and those who are no longer eligible for unemployment benefits. The manufacturing sector has lost *2.7 million* manufacturing jobs since Bush took office. Sure, 9/11 and the trade agreement passed under Clinton's watch had already put us on a slippery slope. But the fact is, as the Bush administration has stood on the sidelines cheering, the good jobs have continued going overseas.

Bush's economic advisor, Greg Mankiw, as quoted in the president's Economic Report to Congress in February 2004, has expressed his philosophy on the problem: "When a good or a service is produced more cheaply abroad, it makes more sense to import it than to make or provide it domestically."

That's only if you don't understand the true cost of the product. What we're sacrificing is the foundation of the country—the working man, the key to a strong economy. A nation isn't purchased. It's built! You need the sweat, brawn, and ingenuity of the working man. And we're losing that at an alarming rate.

An Urban Institute study recently pegged the number of homeless in America as high as 3.5 million in 2000, and according to the National Coalition for the Homeless that number seems to be growing. They say that in twenty-seven U.S. cities, 37 percent of requests for emergency shelter went unmet due to lack of resources—a 13 percent increase from the previous year. More than half of the families seeking help were turned away. In any given year, based on numbers from the Urban Institute, one in one hundred Americans will be homeless. As many as a third of these homeless Americans are veterans.

While growing pains are to be expected in a global marketplace, what has happened to the American worker in recent years is unconscionable. While proponents of the 1994 North American Free Trade Agreement passed on Clinton's watch between America, Canada, and Mexico claimed it would generate 200,000 new American jobs, a more reliable projection came from North Dakota Senator Byron Dorgan, who predicted that it could cost America at least that many jobs. As Dennis Kucinich points out, we've lost more than half a million jobs to NAFTA. One hundred companies alone laid off more than 200,000 workers due to the effects of NAFTA. Among them, in round numbers: *Vanity Fair,* 16,000 jobs; Levi Strauss, 16,000; Burlington House, 10,000; Motorola, 7,000; Tyco, 6,000; General Electric, 6,000; and Fruit of the Loom, 5,000.

One of the great enablers of substandard pay and worse working conditions is Wal-Mart. Wal-Mart used to have signs all over its store reminding customers to "Buy American." What happened to those signs? Here's what happened: Wal-Mart became America's largest importer. According to *Fast Company* magazine, "7.5 cents of every dollar spent in any store in the United States (other than auto parts stores) went to the retailer." And that wasn't enough for the Wal-Mart bean counters. In the race to the bottom line, Wal-Mart decided that low prices override concerns about its workers. Isn't commerce supposed to be *good* for workers? Not when it comes to our great, unaccountable American corporate giants.

This sort of business is vaporizing American jobs, and in China the already oppressed are bearing the burden. In February 2004, the *Washington Post* published a report from Shenzhen, China. Working in an unsafe factory that makes speaker cabinets for Wal-Mart, most of the 2,100 workers are poor migrants who are paid $120 a month. "A sign on the wall reminds them of their expendability in a nation with hundreds of millions of surplus workers: 'If you don't work hard today, tomorrow you'll have to try hard to look for a job.'" Nice morale boost.

"More than 80 percent of the 6,000 factories in Wal-Mart's worldwide database of suppliers are in China. Wal-Mart estimates it spent $15 billion on Chinese-made products last year," the *Post* article continued. In China, of course, labor unions are banned, and low wages are guaranteed. As the *Post* adds, "In the city of Dongguan in southern Guangdong province, where Wal-Mart suppliers are concentrated, a twenty-seven-year-old worker complained that she can rarely afford meat with her $75-per-month wages at Kaida Toy Co. 'Every day we eat vegetables, mostly we eat vegetables,' she said, leaning over a plate of fried carrots in a dingy restaurant. She helps make plastic toy trains for Wal-Mart, but says she cannot afford to buy toys for her nine-year-old son. 'In four years, they haven't increased the salary,' she said.

"Kong Xianghong, the No. 2 official for the party-run union in Guangdong province, acknowledged that low wages, long hours, and poor conditions are common in factories that supply Wal-Mart and other U.S.-based corporations. 'It's better than nothing,' he said."

That's the mindset of the global market: *Take it or leave it.* The big companies figure workers ought to be happy they have a job at all. Better than nothing? Not much.

With somewhere around $250 billion in annual sales, Wal-Mart is the biggest company in the world. Home Depot, number two, does about 25 percent of that amount in sales. There has never been anything quite like Wal-Mart. We are only now starting to sort out the effects of this Frankenstein. As I've been saying for years, I don't darken Wal-Mart's door, because I don't want to feed the monster! Big isn't always bad in business, but when it comes at the expense of moral behavior, it's definitely a horror show.

The Wal-Mart effect shreds small towns. I just can't see how that can be good for our society. I know a little something about small towns. I take my show on the road to these little jewels in America. We attend celebrations all the time. The whole community works hard to put its best foot forward, whether it's a Fourth of July parade, a Little League tournament, or a fishing derby. Up and down Main Street, hometown merchants sponsor softball teams and buy cookies from every Girl Scout. They donate to *everything*. When Wal-Mart swoops into town and wipes out these businesses, are they donating at that level? Are a few pennies saved worth it?

The *Elizabethton Star,* a small newspaper in Tennessee, told one story of local small businesses faced with competition from Wal-Mart. Johnny Mills, owner of Mills Greenhouse in Elizabethton, told the *Star:* "A super Wal-Mart duplicates every job service that we have in this community. It brings not one new product, not one new job, not one new anything to our community. . . . If anybody came in here with a factory or jobs that are not presently in the community, then I think we ought to get a band and go down to the west end of town and lead them into town."

Not only does Wal-Mart kill Mom and Pop stores—and the small towns that rely on them—sometimes Sam Walton's company even eats its own American distributors alive. American companies that sell to Wal-Mart are forced to trim profit margins so close that their workers' wages suffer. Eventually, in order to keep Wal-Mart's crucial business, these American companies find themselves with no choice but to compound the problems of the labor market by shipping their manufacturing jobs overseas themselves.

According to the *Fast Company* report, some time back, struggling Levi Strauss saw Wal-Mart as a way to boost flagging sales. The trouble was, the company didn't have any jeans cheap enough to qualify for Wal-Mart's shelves. So they created a cheaper Signature line of clothing. The strategy worked: It saved the company . . . kind of. Levi Strauss, which once had sixty plants, has now closed its last two U.S. manufacturing plants in San Antonio. Levi Strauss will no longer make jeans: From now on, it will *import* jeans. Levi Strauss may have been suffering before its marketing agreement with Wal-Mart. But Wal-Mart finished it off.

Predictably, Wal-Mart has its defenders. George Will, who has shown a modicum of objectivity with his harsh criticisms of Bush II's handling of the Iraq War, defends Wal-Mart's hold over the economy by pointing out in a *Newsweek* column that the retailer hardly boasts the biggest market share of any American corporation: Wal-Mart may have 8 percent of the retail market, but General Motors has 28 percent—and Anheuser-Busch owns fully *one half* of the American beer market.

Finally, we're in an area of my expertise! The difference is that Budweiser is *brewed in America*. Will never mentions the whole issue of Chinese imports. Anheuser-Busch pays an average brewery worker $49,000 a year. About 7,500 Anheuser-Busch brewery workers are union. Imagine: they're making record profits (an 8 percent increase in 2003) employing union workers in twelve American plants, while growing an international business.

With low Wal-Mart prices, the American consumer wins—at the checkout counter. As Will points out, the big-box discounters keep inflation in check. True enough. But in the long run the American worker isn't really winning at all. After all, consumer and worker are one and the same. I wonder, as middle-class wages stagnate or jobs disappear altogether, who will be left to shop Wal-Mart? As we circle the drain, I'd like to see some clear-eyed economist step up and answer that question.

Levi Strauss isn't the only example of the job exodus initiated by Wal-Mart. Not too long ago, Huffy was America's leading bike manufacturer. Wal-Mart is the number one seller of bikes in America. After Huffy made an agreement to sell its low-end bikes through Wal-Mart, sales exploded. Good, right? Not so. Huffy had to send production orders for more profitable bikes to its competitors, so that it could concentrate on filling orders for those cheap Wal-Mart bikes— and *still* they couldn't keep up. Today, Huffy is the number three seller of bikes in America . . . but Huffy isn't an American brand anymore. Ninety-eight percent of Huffy bikes are now imported.

According to a story in the Idaho *Statesman,* Celina, Ohio, population 9,650, lost a thousand union workers when the Huffy plant moved to Farmington, Missouri, where nonunion workers built bikes for $2.50 less than the $10.50 hourly wage the Ohio union workers earned. (Those who are eager to blame the unions for America's troubles—and there are plenty who do—should look hard at that $10.50 wage. That's less than $22,000 a year. A mid-range house in Celina would cost about $80,000. At $10.50 an hour, that's quite a stretch.)

But even in Missouri they couldn't work cheap enough: The company moved to Mexico—until even Mexican labor proved too expensive. Today, Chinese workers build Huffy bikes . . . for about 4 percent of what Huffy was paying in Ohio.

Huffy is making money. According to the *Statesman,* it went from a $2.2 million loss at the Ohio plant to $35 million in earnings in 2000.

That's great for Wall Street. It's bad for Main Street.

But Main Street doesn't get much consideration from the American CEO, who makes about *250 times* more than an average worker, according to the Economic Policy Institute, a liberal think tank. Huffy CEO Don R. Graber made $1.2 million in 2000, a pretty sizable reward for a year he spent firing American workers.

The American worker isn't on a level playing field. He's more productive than ever—yet health benefits are hard to come by. But damn, you can sure get a real cheap bike at Wal-Mart! Cheer up: With your shrinking paycheck and the ballooning cost of gas, that may be your new ride to work.

When Ross Perot warned us that we were all going to hear a giant sucking sound as American jobs drained over the border to Mexico, who could have imagined that even Mexico would see job losses to China? Even in traditional cheap labor markets in Asia—places like Taiwan, South Korea, Singapore, and Thailand, where working conditions were improving—they're losing jobs to China

According to an October 2003 *USA Today* story, U.S. manufacturing jobs declined from 23 percent in 1987 to 17 percent in 2001.

Americans need to understand that the world is evolving economically, in dramatic fashion. China's thirst for petroleum affects us. Their growing economic power gives them the potential to be the dominant world power in our lifetime. The European Union continues to grow in strength. America may be on top economically now, but we're selling ourselves down the river for the short-term profit of a few. We're living history—and when our grandchildren study how we spent these decades throwing away their legacy, they'll be aghast.

I understand that global trade and a global economy are natural phenomena. But the frenetic pace we're on is leading to disaster. Before we open the doors to more cheap goods, we have to take a long hard look at the impact imports are having on the stability of this country.

This vicious cycle leaves American workers poorer, unable to afford health care or education for college-age children. As more and more uneducated Americans enter the workforce, the average American worker will earn less and less, and the negative cycle is accelerated. Adding insult to injury, families who have been devastated by the squeeze on the working man will be forced to shop Wal-Mart for the low prices, thereby feeding the monster that's a major source of their misery. According to *Forbes* magazine in 2002, five of the top ten wealthiest Americans are from the Walton family.

Maybe we're all just destined to end our lives as Wal-Mart checkers. (It's happening already: One in 115 workers in America works for Wal-Mart.) If that's the case, the company has a responsibility to pay a decent wage and health benefits at its 3,500 stores. When they don't, other Americans pick up the tab for food stamps, Medicaid, and other social programs.

Author Jim Hightower, a staunch opponent of Wal-Mart, points out that the average employee there makes about $15,000 a year. Wal-Mart claims that 70 percent of its 1.2 million employees are full time—but, as Hightower points out, 28 hours a week is considered full time at Wal-Mart.

This is the natural progression of big business in a global economy with few rules. If Kmart had figured out the formula, they would be the monster we're talking about. Wal-Mart just got there first. Today, every other retail operation in the country is under attack from Wal-Mart, which sells more than Kmart, JCPenney, Target, Sears, Safeway, and Kroger combined. So is every community grocery store in the country: Wal-Mart is now the largest grocer in the world.

Hightower sums it up: "By slashing its retail prices way below cost when it enters a community, Wal-Mart can crush our groceries, pharmacies, hardware stores, and other retailers, then raise its prices once it has monopoly control over the market. . . . By crushing local businesses, this giant eliminates three decent jobs for every two Wal-Mart jobs that it creates. Wal-Mart operates as a massive wealth extractor. Instead of profits staying in town to be reinvested locally, the money is hauled off to Bentonville, either to be used as capital for conquering yet another town or simply to be stashed in the family vaults."

Though various government entities are happy to support Wal-Mart, granting at least $1 billion in tax breaks, many average Americans are fighting back. Community after community is opposing the opening of Wal-Mart Supercenters. (The company planned to open a total of 300 new stores in 2004.) Some advocates say an antitrust suit is in order. According to PBS radio, Wal-Mart is the single most sued private business in America—most notably for discrimination against women workers.

I can't imagine what it's like to work there, starting each day with the obligatory pep rally for Wal-Mart: "Go rich guys, Go!" But I have a theory. You know why Wal-Mart stations someone at the door? To tackle any poor "associate" making a break for it! I bet if you check the break room, you'll find a tackling dummy for practice.

As big as Wal-Mart is, it drives the direction of the retail market and the level of wages paid to workers across the country. If the nation's largest employer pays low wages, it forces competitors to cut their wages in an attempt to keep from being run out of business. If the primary family breadwinner is paid $8 an hour at a Wal-Mart checkout counter, how can he or she possibly afford even a co-pay on health insurance? This adds up to a double-bind situation for American workers: While they slave away at the mercy of trade agreements that force them to take jobs that don't cover their health insurance, the cost of health care rises unchecked.

So who wins in this great global-Darwinist marketplace? Multinational corporations. For the multinationals, every new trade agreement is an investment opportunity. And there's another such opportunity for corporations, and another kick in the shorts for workers, just over the horizon: CAFTA. The Central American Free Trade Agreement would involve the United States, Costa Rica, Nicaragua, Guatemala, Honduras, and El Salvador. Again, American businesses will be forced to compete against businesses in poor countries with few labor standards, paying low wages and no benefits.

Senator Byron Dorgan warns that since the impoverished countries involved in CAFTA don't have the wherewithal to purchase American products, CAFTA will again be a one-way street. Dorgan believes it will cost America half a million jobs—and, remember, he was right about NAFTA a decade ago. As Dorgan says, "I don't think we need to be asking U.S. producers to compete with countries where they pay twenty-three cents an hour, hire thirteen-year-olds and dump pollutants freely into the air and water."

The art of global trade is a delicate balance, and it's one we haven't mastered. The answer is prudence. I doubt any economist can tell you with much certainty where all of this is headed. NAFTA sounded like an enlightened idea, but even enlightened ideas can be devastating if they're not fairly administered. We need to proceed more cautiously with future trade agreements. While global trade is undoubtedly the future, we must insist that countries not artificially manipulate the value of their currency to favor their export businesses, as China has done. Too many countries raise the barriers high to keep American merchandise out. Trade has to be a two-way street.

We used to be a nation of builders. We created. We invented. Now, it seems, we have become a nation of consumers. We must restore the balance, or we're in for trouble. Some have expressed the concern that these agreements only elevate third-world economies while ours decline, leaving the two to meet somewhere in the middle. I think the danger is even worse: If we don't do something to save ourselves at home, American workers will meet their third-world competitors at the bottom.

Government by the Rich for the Rich

When it comes to judging our economy, I think a question Ronald Reagan asked in 1980 needs to be asked again: "Are you better off today than you were four years ago?" I'm pretty sure most middle-class Americans would answer with a resounding *"No!"* Americans are working harder, but we're all still going backward. That puts a real strain on the American family. When I start getting e-mails from listeners telling me they have to decide each week between buying gas or buying milk, I start worrying.

I've talked about balance, and balance *is* the key to everything. I see it in my own life. Right now, I'm doing two radio shows—my regional morning show and my afternoon national show. In that respect, I'm a fairly typical American, working his tail off. But I'm doing these shows because I can—and because I feel an obligation to try to restore some balance to the radio airwaves. And the way the conservative talkers have me outnumbered, I feel like a one-legged man in an ass-kicking contest. Yet, it's not like I've got to talk the average American into seeing things my way. I believe working Americans have a sense of the cesspool big business and big government have become.

Many Americans out there are working two jobs because they *have to,* just to pay the bills. If there's anything that captures the distance in this country between the haves and the have-nots, it's just how many full-time jobs don't pay a living wage. A company's race for the almighty dollar easily falls out of balance with its moral obligation to pay workers a decent wage. Some of that is driven by stockholders. I'm a stockholder, too. But I never really understood the excitement many others seem to feel when a Fortune 500 company announces layoffs—and the stock rises at the news! Even I have it figured out that workers fired from decent paying jobs is bad for the economy and the social balance of America, and an America out of balance throws the whole global economy askew.

One day in 2004, I watched Joe Biden fighting for his amendment to raise the top tax bracket by 1 percent for five years to help pay for the war in Iraq. It was just a little give-back from the people who benefited most from the president's $1.6 trillion tax cuts. Biden gave the compelling argument that Americans in the top tax bracket *would* sacrifice if they were asked. "We've just never asked," he said. Thus enlightened, the Republican majority leapt to their feet in agreement, grasped the hands of fellow Senators and began singing *Kumbaya.*

BZZZZ! Wrong. I was just testing to see if you were paying attention.

After Biden's speech, Charles Grassley (R-IA) moaned and groaned and thrashed about so much I thought he might have a stroke. Taking the Republican Party line, he alluded to the supply-side economic theory that inflated the national debt balloon under Reagan and then again under each of the two Bushes. A millionaire himself, Grassley became apoplectic at the thought of giving up *one cent* of the Bush tax cuts.

So what did the Bush team do instead? To subsidize wealthy Americans' tax cuts, this administration dipped $160 billion out of *Social Security.* That's wrong. The wealthy, who won't need Social Security to fall back on, are being subsidized by the common man's retirement fund! Slap on some green tights, Robin Bush, and you and your Merry Henchmen can get back to work robbing from the *poor* and giving to the *rich.*

In 2004, the deficit will be $420 billion. But that's only part of the picture. That doesn't include the $160 billion they're taking from Social Security, which is already on track to be in the red when baby boomers retire. That's why Alan Greenspan advocated Social Security benefits be cut.

Senator Kent Conrad (D-ND), former chairman and ranking Democrat on the Senate Budget Committee, summarized the connection between the tax cuts and the Social Security heist:

> In effect, what is happening here is [that Bush] is taking revenue raised by payroll taxes, paid disproportionately by middle income people and using it to fund income tax cuts for the wealthiest among us. . . . This is truly a remarkable transfer of wealth from the many to the few. He is taking payroll dollars to pay for an income tax that goes to the richest people among us, and the logic of his budget irresponsibility is that the chairman of the Federal Reserve now says you've got to cut Social Security benefits. If that isn't a warning signal on the recklessness of the course the president has taken this country on, I don't know what it will take to convince people.

Let's look back at Ronald Reagan's tax cuts. The top tax rate back then was 70 percent. I agree, that's too high. If I were paying 70 percent, I'd feel like *I* was being punished for being rich. I think that any man or woman who works hard and does well should be able to enjoy the rewards of his or her labors.

But I don't think we ought to give him a *bonus* for being rich. That's what the Bush tax cut did—and it didn't make much sense. When you give a bigger break to the middle class, traditionally it gets spent—dispersed again out into the economy. In fact, unless you followed the tax cut debate closely, you might have missed the fact that the Democrats had just that kind of a tax cut plan on the table—a cut for the *middle class.*

Was the old top tax rate of 38.6 percent, which will be lowered to 35 percent by 2006, out of line? I don't think so. Not when you consider that the median American taxpayer is shelling out around 40 percent of his *total earnings* (depending upon the vagaries of the local tax structure) when you factor in taxes paid on fuel, food, sales, and property taxes, which take a larger percentage of the middle-income family's paycheck than that of a more affluent family.

You can make a strong argument that the middle-class tax burden is *higher* than that of the wealthy. Middle class Americans pay most of their taxes right out of their paychecks for Social Security and Medicare coverage—the programs Bush is gutting to give tax cuts to the wealthy. The bottom 80 percent of households pay only about *28 percent* of their total tax burden in income taxes. The income tax cut is a red herring. It fails to consider the full tax burden of the middle class.

That's why John Kerry's support of a 2002 plan to eliminate *payroll taxes* on the first $10,000 of earnings made sense. It gives the working poor a *real* boost. A two-wage middle-class family would save $1,500. Plus, it encourages new hiring! Here's why: Employers know when they have to calculate the cost of an employee, they must also calculate their business's matching payroll taxes. Less overhead leads to more jobs, and better pay for American workers. It's good for workers, good for employers, good for the economy. Everybody wins.

But didn't those Reagan tax cuts work, you ask?

Well, let's tell the *whole* truth. We all know Reagan drove the public debt to historic heights, leaving a bill you're still paying today. But let's look back at the difference between the Reagan tax cuts and these new Bush tax cuts. Reagan *did* make big cuts; he could afford to. The baby boomers were still a long way from retirement. There was time to make it up. This president, on the other hand, has led us to the brink of financial disaster while proclaiming the predictable short-term bump in the economy as victory.

Mission accomplished, Mr. President?

And there's another thing Reagan did when he saw the tax cuts were leaving the government with huge shortfalls—a little something the Republicans like to forget: he *raised taxes.* Reagan was savvy enough to see he needed to make a mid-course correction by raising corporate and income taxes.

George W. Bush refuses to see the need for any such correction.

Reagan's Social Security Reform Act of 1983 increased payroll taxes. That solidified Social Security and Medicare—but taxes on the middle class actually went up! The Reagan years are not remembered fondly by all social strati. That explains why the Monday after Ronald Reagan's death, when I did a tribute on *The Ed Schultz Show,* so many of my listeners were incensed. They remembered the pounding they took in those years. One carpenter said, "Reagan told me he was going to cut my taxes and he sure did. My income went from $44,000 to $11,000. I was unemployed. I sure paid less in taxes!" I got similar e-mails and phone calls all week long.

It was a little disappointing that a few people weren't able to look beyond their own temporary hardships to appreciate the whole of the man's life on the occasion of his death. I think history will recognize Ronald Reagan as a great president who made some blunders while trying to do good things. But on the other hand, this is what these people experienced in their own lives, and I'm in no position to second-guess that. That day in my Fargo studio was a real eye-opener about the divisiveness in America, which runs so deep that some couldn't pause even a moment before picking at their old wounds.

The response from the anti-Reaganites peeled back a hidden layer of discontent that ran much deeper than I had imagined. When the mourning turned into a GOP reelection commercial, it rubbed many of my listeners the wrong way. They didn't want Bush hijacking any of the goodwill intended for the Gipper.

But I think most Americans are more than angry about the course this administration has embarked upon. I think they're *scared*. Imagine that: In this crown jewel of democracy, many of our citizens fear what our government is going to do next.

And can you blame them? On the eve of the baby boomers' retirement, while the deficits continue to mushroom, Bush robs Social Security. There is little time to pay it back. The plan to fix it? Cut benefits, says Alan Greenspan. Holy smokes! As North Dakota's Kent Conrad has pointed out, *nearly half* of Social Security beneficiaries would be in poverty without Social Security. Don't Americans, whose hard work and tax dollars have built this nation, deserve a modest, secure retirement?

I've been puzzled at all this insane spending by the Bush administration. A quick review: Clinton left Bush II a financial house in such good order that the national debt would have been retired within a decade. Then you have 9/11 . . . and Bush takes the opportunity to hammer home $1.6 trillion in tax cuts for the rich. A $540 trillion payoff to drug manufacturers disguised as a social program. Two wars on two fronts. It's a financial train wreck about to happen.

What's wrong with this picture? Well, for one thing, it's all one big role reversal. Ask anyone in America who the "Tax and Spend" party is supposed to be, and they'll say "the Democrats." But look back, and you'll realize that almost all of the $7 trillion national debt we now carry was created under three administrations: Reagan, Bush I, and Bush II. Bill Clinton, standard-bearer for the Democrats, *paid down the debt.*

I'm starting to believe that the unspoken platform of the Republican Party was to dismantle the New Deal's social programs by purposely breaking the bank!

That sounds a little paranoid, right? Well, consider this passage from Noam Chomsky's *Hegemony or Survival*:

Government deficits require 'fiscal discipline,' which translates into cutbacks for services for the general population. The administration's own economists estimate the bills the government will be unable to pay at $44 trillion. [Author's note: The net worth of the country is estimated at $42 trillion.] Their study was to be included in the annual budget published in February 2003 but was removed, perhaps because it forecast that closing the gap would require a huge tax increase and Bush was trying to ram through another tax reduction, again benefiting mainly the rich. *'President Bush is working overtime to deepen the our fiscal trap,' economists Laurence Kotlikoff and Jeffrey Sachs observe, reporting the enormous anticipated fiscal gap. Among the results, they contend, will be 'massive cuts in future Social Security and Medicare benefits.'* White House Spokesperson Ari Fleischer agreed with the $44 trillion estimate and implicitly conceded the accuracy of the analysis as well: 'There is no question that Social Security and Medicare are going to present (future) generations with a crushing debt burden unless policymakers work to seriously reform those programs'—which does not mean funding them by progressive taxation. The problem is deepened by the serious financial crisis of states and cities.

The editors of the staid *Financial Times* are only 'stating the obvious,' economist Paul Krugman comments [Author's note: *New*

York Times, 2003], when they write that the 'more extreme Republicans' with their hands on the controls seem to want a fiscal train wreck that offers 'the tantalizing prospect of forcing (cuts on social programs) through the back door.' Stated for demolition, Krugman contends, are Medicaid, Medicare and Social Security, but the same may be true for the whole range of programs of the past century that were developed to protect the population from the ravages of private power.

This is class warfare—and it's been declared on you. The agenda is to create an impervious, untouchable wealthy class, and a powerless peasant class.

And make no mistake about it: this is just as bad for the Republican middle class as it is for the Democrats.

The Bushies are like street hustlers. While they're showing you a meager tax cut with one hand, they're stealing your wallet with the other. No matter how you shuffle the bills around, ultimately those bills have got to be paid. And the national debt bills we're putting off today are going to fall to our children to pay. And our personal checkbooks are no better than the government's: The average American child is born into a household with an average debt load of $45,000. The squeeze is so tight, personal savings have fallen from nearly 9 percent of our income in 1984 to 0.5 percent in 1998.

Still, the neocons continue to heap insult on injury. They flimflam the public into believing the estate tax (the "Death Tax," as they call it) affects middle America. It does not! The estate tax doesn't tax people who *earned* it. It taxes people with rich daddies. I don't think there's a problem with parents trying to give their kids a little something for the road. But when the country's wealth is unduly concentrated—wealth unearned—it throws off the balance of the country. You end up with a large aristocracy and an even larger group of have-nots. "The richest 1 percent of the population now owns as much wealth as the bottom 95 percent of all Americans combined," reports Vermont Independent Congressman Bernie Sanders. These are the people getting the tax breaks.

In 2002, economist Paul Krugman said in the *New York Times*:

> The most remarkable example of how politics has shifted in favor of the wealthy is the drive to repeal the estate tax. In 1999, only the top 2 percent of estates paid any tax at all. . . . It is no accident that strongly conservative views, views that militate against taxes on the rich, have spread even as the rich get richer: in addition to directly buying influence, money can be used to shape public perceptions.

Do you want to know the dirty secret about the real reason Bush gives tax cuts to the rich? It's simple: Most middle Americans don't donate big money to political campaigns. They don't have it to give. Rich people donate because they expect to get something in return, like the ear of the vice president during energy policy decisions. You want service from this administration? You have to pay for it.

The estate tax is a balancing mechanism recognized by governments as far back as ancient Egypt. But even in the heartland, the fear of a death tax provokes shrill cries of opposition. According to the Brookings Institution, in 1997 "farm assets totaled a microscopic 0.3 percent of taxable estates . . . Only 3 percent of estates consist mainly of farms or small business." Plus, there are special protections to allow transfer of farms to the next generation.

Once again, conservatives stampeded middle Americans into supporting a tax cut for the rich with scare tactics. These people could incite a panic at a swimming pool by yelling "Fire!" Get real. The federal estate tax exemption is $1.5 million. If you're worried about paying estate taxes, you're probably not reading this book.

Mahatma Gandhi said, "There are seven sins in the world: wealth without work, pleasure without conscience, knowledge without morality, commerce without morality, science without humanity, worship without sacrifice, and politics without principle." Looks like the Bushies are batting 1.000.

Money is power. It buys politicians. It buys elections. Think about it: Forty U.S. senators are officially millionaires. The actual number is certainly higher, because these financial statements grant senators a good deal of wiggle room. You think you live in a democracy? You're governed by aristocrats. You almost have to be a rich person, or have rich friends, to win. Why? Because advertising works. Slick thirty-second ads affect the way people feel about candidates. A great ad campaign can trump almost anything. And once you're in, it's tough to get you out again.

In 2000, 98.5 percent of House incumbents won their races. It's an old story. Going back fifty years, the reelection rate for incumbents in the U.S. House has remained at 90 percent or higher, except for the anti-Nixon election of 1974—when 89.6 percent of the incumbents won.

Campaign finance reform must be an ongoing process. But the big change has to come from the broadcast industry. We are licensed by the Federal Communications Commission to use the public airwaves not just for profit—but for the public good. I say we mandate equal time for candidates on radio and television. Broadcasters will kick about the lost advertising revenue, but let's be honest here: That's gravy. We don't live and die over election revenue. Broadcasters should not just take. They must give back, too. As a nation, we must demand that broadcasters operate for the public good, as is their mandate, and not strictly as a money machine.

You want to get the money out of politics? Equal time would be a good start.

Money buys a lot of things in our culture. It can buy you a not-guilty verdict. It can buy you a better education. No matter how you 'nice it up,' that's the bottom line. But you don't hear that message—or if you do, it's muted, because of the increasing consolidation of the media by—you guessed it—the wealthy.

This country was founded by immigrants fleeing aristocracies. They came to America inspired by the dream of equality. In the heart of the Dakotas, we are barely a generation removed from rugged men and women who escaped poverty in Europe and tyranny in Russia for 160 acres of prairie and a fair chance to make a go of it. A basic principle, in the grand race of capitalism, was that we all start with relatively equal opportunity. May the best and brightest win.

I still believe in Horatio Alger. I still think America is the land of opportunity. Even a jockstrap like me can make it with hard work. But the doors of opportunity are closing.

Greed, in any system, kills it. You need balance. When any of the Four Pillars is weakened, like the Second Pillar—a sound economy—the whole structure is endangered.

According to Congressman Sanders, between 1973 and 1997, the average incomes of the poorest 20 percent of families fell by 5 percent. The richest 20 percent, on the other hand, saw their advantage grow by 41 percent. Globally, this growing gap between the haves and have-nots has led us to a point when the richest 225 people in the world own assets equal to 47 percent of the entire world's population.

The world of the post–World War II generation, which saw a boom in the middle class, is not the same world we live in today, which finds many families just getting by on two incomes. We work harder. We work longer. We shuffle the kids off to daycare. And slowly the social fabric of family and society around us unravels.

Conservatives can talk about family values all they want, but they can shoulder some of the blame for it, too. Their policies are kicking working Americans repeatedly in the hind end, by stealing away overtime pay and allowing corporations to send jobs overseas with no penalty, which is nothing more than union-busting by another name. The middle class is being saddled with mountains of debt our children will have to pay. We're being drawn into wars our children will have to fight. But the neocons don't care. It doesn't matter to them.

Health Care Costs
Threaten the Economy

A t first blush, the topic of health care might not seem to fit under the umbrella of "sound economy." But affordable health care is more than just a frill, a fringe benefit for the lucky among us. I believe with all my heart that this is a make-or-break issue for the economic health of middle America, and therefore for America itself.

I don't believe in the word *can't*. I don't think most Americans much care for the word, either. America has *always* been able to find grand solutions for big problems. That has been, and continues to be, one of the defining trademarks of Americans. When we say we're going to the moon, we do it. When we say, "Tear down this wall," we mean it.

So why can't we solve the health care crisis in America? Forty-four million Americans cannot afford health insurance from an industry that metes out double-digit increases annually.

According to *USA Today*, health insurance premiums were up 13.9 percent in 2003. From 2000 to 2003, workers' co-pay of family coverage provided by employees increased from $1,600 to $2,400. Out-of-pocket expenses for prescriptions increased between 46 percent and 71 percent. Employers saw their company plans escalate in price from $6,400 to $9,000, a 41 percent increase over three years! Small businesses had even higher increases. For large businesses, the option of sending jobs overseas just gets easier. For small businesses, there are two options: freeze wages or cut benefits.

If it's not a crisis now, when will it be? When fifty million Americans are without health insurance? Seventy million? Seventy-five million? These aren't just numbers we're talking about. These are living, breathing, suffering human beings. At long last, don't we have to take a serious look at universal health care?

We shouldn't have to look far. Our neighbors to the north in Canada have a successful health care system. I've had Canadian listeners and callers for years. I've gotten anecdotal arguments pro and con. But even if it's not perfect, ask yourself, what government program is? Perfection never happens in a democracy—as evidenced by our current health care mess. I know we talk about having the best health care in the world, but what good does it do when patients are put at risk because they can't afford the best care?

The World Health Organization reports that Americans pay twice as much per capita for health as the average industrialized nation. Doug Garr, a New York City writer, recently published an essay in *Newsweek* that profoundly illustrated the difference between health care in various industrialized nations. Doug's wife suffered a stroke in France. When Doug asked for an itemized statement for the two-and-a-half-week stay for his insurance company in America, he got a simple one-page bill. No extra charges. There were only two rates—one for intensive care and one for nonacute care.

When the Garrs got home, they were swamped with paperwork, receiving bills from doctors they'd never heard of, let alone seen. The billing was rife with mistakes. Doug discovered what he was experiencing was common. Probably the norm. Of the $300,000 total he was eventually billed, $90,000 had nothing to do with patient care. Roughly 30 percent of each health care dollar, he wrote, goes toward paperwork.

In previous chapters, I've talked about the conservative philosophy of privatizing just about everything. Health care is a real sacred cow because it makes money. But is privatization always more efficient? As Garr says, "Medicare—our government subsidized system that cares for the elderly—has a much better record in administrative costs. It spends between three and four cents of every dollar on paperwork."

I've probably created a medical emergency for many of my readers who fainted dead away with the discovery of government efficiency! Garr sums up his story by saying, "A single payer-system is easier and cheaper to run. We've had a two-tier health care system in the United States for a while, and only one tier works."

I know Americans are not refused care during an emergency. But they still get that $50,000 bill. Medical bills lead to bankruptcies and very real family hardships. According to a 2004 report from the Center for Studying Health System Change, nearly 20 million American families—one in seven—had trouble paying medical bills in 2003. Two-thirds of those cash-strapped families have health insurance!

According to a recent story in *Investor's Business Daily*, "median weekly earnings have been rising a paltry 0.7 percent per year since 1993 while total income has grown an annual 1.7 percent in the last decade, according to inflation-adjusted government data." Wages have stagnated while health care costs have gone through the roof. If that isn't a recipe for disaster, I don't know what is.

I want to tell you how it is in every small town in rural America. When some poor unfortunate is stricken with a potentially terminal illness and can't pay the bills, church groups and scout troops hold car washes and bake sales to raise money. If there's a symbol of the failure of our system, it's the coffee can on the counter at the local cafe, collecting nickel-and-dime donations to help the family pay the bills.

We have a coffee-can health care system in America. Drive across the heartland. Stop at any cafe. You'll see a hundred hard-luck stories of mothers dying, children orphaned, or worse, the smiling faces of toddlers with cancer. Man, I've stuffed more coffee cans with dollar bills than I can remember. So many good Americans want to give. But when it comes to a national health care plan, they listen to the Republican drumbeat and forget about these human stories.

Tom Daschle—who is truly one of the most decent men I've ever met—tells the story of Lowell and Pauline Larson from Chester, South Dakota. "Throughout their life together, Lowell and Pauline farmed a hundred and sixty acres just outside of Chester, South Dakota. After a lifetime of hard work, they were looking forward to a well-earned retirement together. But two years ago, Pauline suffered a stroke. Before the Larsons knew it, they had incurred $40,000 in medical bills. Even though they had insurance, it only covered $75 a day of Pauline's hospital costs. So Lowell did the only thing he could. He sold all his farm equipment and his cattle to pay the bills. All they are left with is the deed to their farm, and if Pauline suffers another stroke, or if the MS she has been battling for the past fifteen years gets worse, the Larsons know they may have to sell their farm. We need to reject the notion that the primary purpose of our health care system is to provide profits for health care companies and the drug industry. That is wrong. That is the thinking that brought us to the point where families such as the Larsons are forced to turn over the proceeds of their life's work, just to pay the bill for treating a single illness."

The bills get paid one way or another. You know who pays when someone defaults? You guessed it. You. Insurance premiums continue to rise, forcing more Americans to go without insurance, escalating the negative cycle.

There has been some talk in the past of mandating that employers offer health insurance. I don't see it working. It would kill small businesses, even those who *want* to offer their loyal employees insurance. Many of them just can't afford it.

There's always talk in Congress about doing this or that to help American businesses. Here's a big one. You want to see hiring go through the roof and wages increase? Just take that health insurance line item out of the company budget. A universal plan would be a boon to employers and, most important, employees. Conservatives seem to view health care as a luxury item. But in America, I still believe our people deserve to have the basic necessities—food, shelter, education, and health care. It's the decent thing to do. If Canada can do it, America can do it.

Oh, I can hear the fear-mongering starting already. *Oh, but the health care is substandard! There'll be endless waits for your crucial gizzard transplant!* Really? Will all you medical experts please explain why Canada, according to 2004 Central Intelligence Agency estimates, has a higher life expectancy—79.96 years to America's 77.43? Only eleven countries rank higher than Canada.

The best is Andorra, where life expectancy is at 83.5 years. I think it would be fun for reporters to ask President Bush who the leader of Andorra is. Okay, just so it doesn't drive you crazy wondering, Andorra is a democracy that borders France and Spain. It has a population of seventy thousand, and—drum roll, please—*no income tax!* No, Mr. President, I'm not going to tell you who the leader of Andorra is. I *will* say they'll be easy to invade if they start getting lippy.

Infant mortality in Canada is the twenty-third lowest in the world. America, home of the best health care money can buy (and that's the problem) ranks forty-first, two places behind Cuba's infant mortality rate of 6.45 per thousand births. The United States stands at 6.63 per thousand.

So much for the inferior Canadian health care system.

As Doug Garr pointed out in *Newsweek,* American health care is inefficient. While many hospitals struggle, some HMOs are rolling in dough. As a business, an HMO charges what the market will bear—and the price doesn't necessarily have anything to do with actual costs. *Mother Jones* magazine looked at the way an appendectomy in the Detroit area was billed. A Blue Cross HMO charged about $5,000 for the procedure; Medicare was charged about $6,000 for the same operation. So how did a person too poor to afford insurance fare? He got a $15,000 bill! Talk about kicking you when you're down.

And in Canada? An uninsured American would pay less than $2,000 for the same operation.

Singapore has the lowest infant mortality rate in the world—2.28 percent. The worst place to live? Botswana (and AIDS- and war-ravaged Africa in general). Life expectancy in Botswana is 30.76 years. One of the stains on Ronald Reagan's legacy is that his administration did nothing when it could have done so much so early to stop the spread of AIDS, which today is virtually wiping out a continent. The World Health Organization estimates that forty million people are infected with HIV. Three million people died of AIDS in 2003. We can do better—abroad and at home. This is a moral issue, the kind the Republicans are usually so good at talking about. Where are you compassionate conservatives, anyway?

I'll tell you: They're feeling a little under the weather. Just try mentioning universal health care to a few Republicans, and see if they don't all start flopping around like a crappie out of water. But universal health care is a big idea whose time has come. So was Social Security. So were the New Deal and Roosevelt's WPA projects. We can do it. Yes, it will have an impact on our national budget and our tax rate. I don't see any way around that. But I believe that in the long run it will boost the economy. Heck, my theory is at least as valid as trickle-down economics. As a nation we already pay—one way or another—for health care. Universal health care is a more equitable approach.

Think about it: With all those national health care costs to float, are Canadians paying significantly more than Americans in taxes? Canada's provincial taxes are higher than most American state taxes, but Canadians pay less (as a percentage) in federal taxes than we do. Americans also get mortgage deductions, which Canadians do not. It seems to me that we're not all that far apart.

According to an April 2004 *MSN Money* story by Jeff Wurio, America ranks twenty-eighth out of thirty industrialized nations in its federal tax burden. As Wurio reports, American tax revenue is only 26 percent of our gross domestic product. Sweden, on the other hand, tops the chart, collecting 52 percent of its gross domestic product in taxes; they also have one of the world's highest per-person incomes—$32,000, compared to the United States at $28,500. Base income taxes in Sweden start at 32 percent.

Norway has the world's highest per-person annual income— nearly $40,000—and a federal tax/GDP ratio of 42 percent. Norway provides its citizens with free daycare, health care reimbursement for costs exceeding about $180, education through graduate school, forty-two weeks of maternal leave with full pay (compared to twelve for U.S. workers) and a month annual vacation—not as good as President Bush, but better than most Americans ever manage.

But before we give the government all of our money, the *MSN Money* story also tells a cautionary tale. Companies in these countries spend 60 percent less than American counterparts on research and development. The story quotes Doug Shackelford, a University of North Carolina accounting professor and European tax expert. "You definitely find less entrepreneurial activities," he says. "The thinking is, 'What's the use of it?'"

Clearly, that stagnation is the fear of most conservatives. And I feel the same way. But while these countries have swung too far to the left and stifled innovation in favor of social programs, America remains too far to the right when it comes to administering a dignified brand of basic health care to all.

Our system is broken. We have to fix it. We must strike a balance. I'm not talking about making health care a total freebie. What I *am* talking about is making it affordable!

Congressman Dick Gephardt (D-MO) laid out a health care plan in the Democratic primaries that would cost $2 trillion over ten years to cover forty million people. Look, I know we need to save up for Bush's next invasion, but couldn't we dig under the couch cushions a little bit? If we can manage to squirrel away a few hundred billion here, a few hundred billion there, pretty soon we'll be talking some real money.

We can do this! America has always been a land of big ideas.

These days, we're acting like we're just the home of big profits.

America's new Prescription Drug Bill was a disappointing and expensive remedy, calculated for political gain. The Republicans took a longtime Democratic wish, and bastardized the plan to serve its own special-interest pals. Jim DeMint, a Republican Congressman from South Carolina, blasted the bill and the GOP for turning its back on fiscal conservatism. "At a time of war and record federal deficits," he said, "the nation cannot afford this vast expansion of Medicare. The benefit eventually will cover about 75 percent of seniors' drug expenses up to $2,250, with generous subsidies above that figure as well . . . Congress blithely refused to pay for the drug benefit up front, opting instead to add the cost to the deficit for future generations to pay. Politics clearly was the motive behind the excessive size of the drug plan. By voting for the plan, congressional Republicans shored up the senior citizen vote for next year—but at the cost of Republican principles."

Drug companies fought the bill because they feared a forty million person buying bloc would drive down prices. The VA and Medicaid programs buy drugs at a 40 percent discount. (Note: Medicaid is a combined federal/state program that provides health services for low-income individuals and families and is the primary payer of nursing home care. Medicare is strictly a federal health insurance program for the elderly and the disabled. People who qualify for Social Security benefits are eligible for Medicare.)

Here's the problem: *The new drug bill does not allow the government to negotiate prices.* This was made possible by our legalized system of bribery. Pharmaceutical companies spent $20 million on congressional races in 2002—and 80 percent of that on Republicans. Well, they certainly got what they paid for. According to a *USA Today* story in July 2003, drug makers also spent $17 million on a TV ad campaign to help elect Republicans in tight races. Drug companies spent $91 million on 675 lobbyists in 2002, *USA Today* reports. Holy smokes! That's enough to have one for every person in the U.S. House and Senate, with dozens left over to woo the White House.

Ultimately, does the bill help seniors? Theoretically, yes—if anyone can figure it out. They spent so much selling this lemon, they forgot to teach anyone how to drive it! With more seniors covered, more prescriptions will be filled at full price. It's a very good deal for drug companies. A good deal for senior citizens. But it is a wasteful plan.

Canada has a price-controls board that keeps drugs affordable. (The Canadian health plan does not cover prescriptions.) As a result, Canadians pay 40 percent to 50 percent less for most of the same drugs Americans take. So why do the drug companies charge their American consumers so much more? *Because they can.* They charge what they believe the market will bear.

According to an ABC News report, a prescription for the cancer drug Campath that costs $2,400 in America costs $660 for Canadians. How many Americans don't take life-saving medications because they can't afford them? Doctors will tell you it happens all the time. Some kindly old woman can't afford her blood pressure medication, and the next thing you know . . . *Boom* . . . a stroke. Medicaid kicks in—and *you* pick up the bill.

This price gouging is immoral. Just as immoral is a government that refuses to stop it because its members have been bought off. Some rural Democrats provided swing votes on the bill because it helped fund strapped rural hospitals. Our rural hospitals receive a lower Medicare reimbursement for the same services provided in urban hospitals. Many rural hospitals are in danger of closing because of inequities in Medicare reimbursement. In rural areas people die because they cannot get to adequate medical care quickly enough. When a rural hospital closes, it doesn't just devastate the community economically; it also jeopardizes lives that could have been saved.

I know Democrats want to go back to fix the inequities and flaws in the drug bill. Bush *knew* the bill would cost more than the proposed $400 billion. But he kept the real figure—$540 billion more—hidden until the bill was passed.

And get a load of the Bush plan for health insurance. He wants middle Americans, who have been ravaged by his economic nihilism, to somehow find a way to save money in a Medical Savings Account that they have not been able to do otherwise.

There's a guy who's out of touch with the real world.

Maybe one of the cruelest ironies to come from Ronald Reagan's funeral is that while the conservatives were willing to glory in Reagan's accomplishments, they muffled debate on the stem cell research Nancy Reagan was pleading for. The great tragedy of Ronald Reagan's life was that he never got to enjoy the accolades he deserved, or to contribute to the political process in his postpresidency. If Reagan had been active throughout the 1990s, I fully believe that the political divisiveness we experience today would have been lessened.

I know exactly what Nancy Reagan went through. I watched the decline of my mother as she struggled with Alzheimer's disease. She slowly drifted away—a woman who had been so sharp, such a vibrant part of my life. During the years I lived in North Dakota, when I went home to see Mom in Norfolk, she would leap out of her chair and embrace me. In her last year, when Mom was in an assisted living facility, Wendy and I went back to see her. She was eating when we arrived. I touched her shoulder and said, "Hi, Mom . . ." She looked up at me for a moment. Time stopped. And then she looked back down at her plate and began eating again. Do you know how that feels?

The hope of stem cell research is that Alzheimer's disease may be cured and the paralyzed may walk again. But that hope appears to have fallen on deaf ears in the Bush camp.

On my show one day, I got a moving call from a paralyzed woman who implored Bush to remove the limitations on stem cell research. I also heard from Cheri Gunvalson of Gonvick, Minnesota, whose son, Jacob, suffers from a terminal form of muscular dystrophy, another disease that might be cured with stem cell research. Later, Cheri shared with me a letter she sent to Norm Coleman (R-MN), the senator who won the election in Minnesota after Paul Wellstone's death in a plane crash.

"Expanding the number of available stem cell lines may prove to be a vital tool in allowing scientists to fully develop the promise of stem cell research," Cheri wrote. She went on to explain to Coleman that there were only fifteen viable stem cell lines available, which drastically limits research opportunities.

"Personally, I would never have an abortion," Cheri continued. "However, I would donate any part of my body, including my unused eggs, to save my son. I ask you, do you believe in fertility clinics where they mass-produce millions of five-day old blastocys that are going in the garbage, but are unwilling to use [them] to save our sons? My friend, Mary, is a staunch Catholic and is infertile. She does not believe in fertility clinics, so she and her husband have adopted two lovely boys. Mary would give any part of her body to save her sons, including her unused eggs. Mary is for stem cell research; what mother would be against it? This is not abortion. This is as pro-life as you can get!"

Bush's stand against expanding stem cell research is a political one, designed to preserve the votes of the fundamentalist right. I can't believe God would choose cells in a petri dish over a living, breathing, and suffering human being.

I thought back to the day I saw the New England Patriots receiver Darryl Stingley paralyzed on the football field when I was a free agent with the Oakland Raiders. I was on the sidelines at an exhibition game on August 12, 1978, when Jack Tatum collided helmet to helmet with Stingley. It was a violent hit. As the raucous crowd went silent, Stingley, who had stretched out for a pass, lay crumpled on the ground, forever paralyzed. Raider crowds are notoriously brutal, but that day you could have heard a pin drop. An exhibition game had become a life or death drama.

Today, there is new hope for Stingley's recovery. Stem cell research is offering researchers hope that they may be able to regenerate spinal tissue. Research continues around the world. And yet in America, the best researchers are essentially being asked to sit this one out. What we need is a Manhattan Project for stem cell research. Having mustered the will to create tools of destruction, why not, just this once, do the same in an effort to heal? After a quarter-century in a wheelchair, Darryl Stingley would love to walk again.

And Jacob Gunvalson wants to live.

DEFENDING AMERICA SOLUTIONS

- *Big business corruption:* Much of the problem concerns the connections between big business and the highest level of government. We need an Ethics Czar every bit as much as we need an Anti-terrorism Czar. The conflicts of interest between business and government must be ended. Just as this country is founded on the separation of church and state, we must preserve the separation of industry and government.

   The current administration has many questions to answer on this score—especially Dick Cheney. It's fine for a businessman to be a government leader. But government shouldn't be a business opportunity. The SEC needs to grow a spine and severely punish corporate misdeeds that shake the economy. The American investor has lost faith in American businesses. We need another Teddy Roosevelt and get him out there busting up monopolies. Monopolies kill capitalism and democracy.

Change could come overnight if someone like the owners of Wal-Mart decided they could live with merely hundreds of millions, instead of billions, and set an example by paying fair wages, benefits and improving working conditions in the factories that manufacture their products. Wouldn't you shop at a company that was doing the right thing?

The justice system must be overhauled—and I'm not talking about tort reform or a $250,000 cap on damages. Americans must have some legal recourse against big corporations. Our court system favors monied interests which can legally and financially destroy a litigant even if he is right. In America today, politicians and justice itself are for sale. Democracy cannot long survive this inequity.

- *Outsourcing:* I agree with the plan of leading Democrats to reward businesses for keeping American jobs in America. Historically, this is a Republican philosophy, and I think it shows a real level of sincerity on the part of the Democrats to part with their old philosophies and promote it today. As a consumer, here's what you can do: Support businesses who support America. I'm not talking about extreme protectionism. The reality is we have a global market. We have to make it work for everyone. But when you get a chance to buy American, do. Support labor unions. Don't cross picket lines. These guys are protecting even nonunion jobs by setting a reasonable standard for the treatment of the American worker. A global minimum wage will level the playing field for American businesses somewhat, and it will improve the lives of the poor workers in Asia who produced the goods.

- *The wealth gap:* While I don't think a return to the days of a 90 percent (or even 70 percent) top tax bracket makes sense, we have to come to grips with the dire nature of the debt and deficit. Giving huge tax breaks to the wealthy serves no other purpose than to garner votes. We must balance the budget so that we'll be able to afford Social Security in perpetuity. We have to stop privatizing everything government does.

Think of it this way: Mercenaries never win wars, because they're fighting for a paycheck, not for their country. The same goes for the corporate interests in Washington: They're out for themselves, not for America. Our wealthy upper class is only growing more powerful, and history proves that power that hasn't been earned is a dangerous thing. We need to reinstate the estate tax, to help balance the effects of inherited wealth. And let's look at entitlements. Wasn't the original intent of Social Security and Medicare to help the poor and middle class have a dignified life and retirement? Why not base payments on the median wage? As your net worth rises, you should receive a diminishing Social Security and Medicare benefit. According to Peter G. Peterson, former Secretary of Commerce and author of *Running on Empty,* the elderly have a lower poverty rate (10.4 percent) than any other age group. Let's concentrate on helping those who really need it. In the heartland, many of those people *are* elderly. We can be fiscally responsible and do the right thing for the right people.

- *Health care:* We *have* to succeed on this one. This is a very basic moral issue. It speaks to who we are. Let's recall Emma Lazarus's inspiring lines engraved on the pedestal of the Statue of Liberty:

Give me your tired, your poor,
Your huddled masses yearning to breathe free,
The wretched refuse of your teeming shore.
Send these, the homeless . . .

Today in America, the poor, huddled masses are no exotic import: They're our own people. The health care industry has to get its own house in order to extend care to these people, or the government has to step in and do it for them. Poor and middle-class Americans—*and that's what this is all about*—deserve the basic dignity of decent, affordable health care. We need to concentrate on preventative medicine.

Americans need to get off their posteriors and go for a walk once in a while. We need to donate blood. To list ourselves as organ donors on our driver's licenses. To sign up to be a bone marrow donor.

We need to start saving each other's lives.

THE THIRD PILLAR

FEEDING THE NATION

THE PROBLEM

I've devoted many pages to the first two pillars—defense and the economy—because America is at the cusp of a major disaster in those areas. The next two pillars, food supply and education, are looming crises of a different kind. For the heartland, the challenges to our agricultural base are crises we experience daily. We are losing our family farms and with them our small towns. Global food companies like Cargill have a presence in seventy countries. We are seeing companies like these gain a monopoly over the food industry. Trade agreements have hurt not only American workers, but farmers, too.

But protectionism has devastated more than just our own heartland. Emerging economies have suffered far more than ours. These countries can't compete with the subsidies other industrialized nations give their farmers, and the result is often starvation. Capitalism has produced inequities when it comes to food distribution. Not to mention the effect of wars and corrupt regimes—the greatest cause of starvation.

HOW DOES THIS AFFECT ME?

Here's the thing about human beings: We can live without gasoline, telephones, even television or (say it ain't so!) radio. We *can't* live without food. As we have seen in our chapter on the First Pillar—defense—our dependence on oil has led America into some unhealthy political situations. An oil monopoly governs us and the actions of our country. Now, imagine what would happen if there were to be an absolute monopoly on food, from the field to the store shelf.

It could happen. Prices would rise as quality fell. It happens whenever there is no competition. It's happening today. It's bad for farmers and bad for you.

Your Grocery Bill Is Subsidized, for Now

Nowhere in the world can a citizen eat so well for so little as in America. But those days may well be coming to an end. For as America loses its family farmers, not only are we losing the soul of the heartland, but silently, our food supply is being monopolized.

Why did Teddy Roosevelt (who spent a good deal of time ranching in North Dakota) bust up monopolies? Because they're economic dictatorships. When a monopoly takes control of a market, prices go up. Quality goes down. And people get hurt.

A few years ago, when I took my blinders off and started realizing what the American farmer was up against, I realized that he's an endangered species. Farmers are disappearing like the Plains horseman.

And, tragically, the loss of the American family farm has been accelerated by government policy and reckless trade agreements.

Today, the American farmer is the most efficient producer in the world. What's his reward for efficiency? He has to work even harder, to be even more productive, just to break even. The problem is, he's not on a level playing field. Not only do other developed countries subsidize their farmers dramatically, distorting the marketplace, but the American farmer is at the mercy of a few global corporations who can pick and choose the cheapest prices from those unfairly subsidized markets.

The inequities are startling. Consider: European Union countries subsidize their farmers $309 per acre. According to the House Agriculture Committee, the U.S. subsidizes American farmers just $49 an acre. The result is that the American farmer is forced to sell his goods in a global marketplace shaped by artificially depressed prices—prices that often dip below the cost of production!

American farmers have seen their interests traded away by our own negotiators, who seem more concerned with paving the way for American banking interests abroad and making sure that Wal-Mart gets plenty of cheap foreign-made widgets in time for the holiday season.

Not only is the American farmer at a cost-of-production disadvantage, he's also facing world markets that are often effectively closed. On average, foreign tariffs are currently hovering at about 62 percent, while U.S. tariffs are about 12 percent!

Why do European countries defend their farmers so staunchly? It's because they've experienced hunger and starvation far worse than the United States did during the Great Depression. They understand the Third Pillar in Big Ed's Four Pillars of a great nation: *You've got to feed the nation!* America has never really been scarred by starvation, so we don't pay much attention to food policy—in just the same way that we ignored the dangers of terrorism until 9/11.

When you get right down to it, capitalism has a spotty record of feeding the world. There's enough food; it's just going to the highest bidder. According to CARE, twenty-three starving children die every minute. In 2002, there were thirty-two countries with severe hunger issues. Twenty-one countries faced food shortages triggered by drought and other poor weather. Eight nations attributed the starvation to a combination of weather and economic strife. Fifteen countries endured hunger because of war, some in combination with weather and other issues.

Europe's extreme agricultural subsidies are not only hurting the American farmer, they're hurting farmers in these emerging markets, whose countries can't afford subsidies.

The American farmer *can* compete and win, but the deck is stacked against him. The number of buyers is limited. Three companies—Archer Daniels Midland, Cargill, and Continental control *80 percent* of the world's grain shipments.

When markets are controlled by a few companies, is that bad? Not in theory. Corporations have the power to do great things. They build planes and computers and cars. They make our lives better in many ways. There is an efficiency of scale at work here. It's simple mathematics. But as I've said, a powerful company, like a powerful nation, has the potential to do just as much harm as it does good.

It's about balance. Power must be balanced by a sense of moral purpose. This is the greediest generation ever to walk this land, and that greed demands higher profits on Wall Street. That enormous pressure on these companies amplifies ruthlessness. Profit begins to override any moral sensibility.

Materialism is unhealthy. We shouldn't get too attached to *things*. But detachment from materialism ought to be a choice. In middle America, conservatives are making it mandatory—by taking away our ability to better our lives. They're giving breaks to the wealthy—those of us who are more *experienced* with materialism. I guess it's for our own good. We probably couldn't *handle* affluence. But it would be nice to try.

William D. Heffernan, Ph D, Professor of Rural Sociology at the University of Missouri–Columbia, says that when markets are controlled by only a few buyers, it gives the buyers disproportionate economic power. "If an individual farmer has reasonable access to only one buyer or seller, the farmer must continue that economic relationship by accepting *almost any* contractual terms the food firm offers," said Heffernan in his 1999 Report to the National Farmers Union, "Consolidation in the Food and Agriculture System."

Even though farmers endure soaring costs of fuel, seed, and labor, they must still accept what the only buyers are willing to pay. When the farmer must sell grain below the cost of production, subsidies kick in so he can keep going another year—in theory.

According to the House Agriculture Committee, the 2002 Farm Bill costs each person a mere thirteen cents a day. What's the return on that thirteen cents? While in developing nations, people may spend *half* of their income on food, American families spend a paltry 10 percent of their income on food (including restaurant dining), as compared to 20 percent in the 1960s. The farmer gets little of it. In 2000, according to the Rocky Mountain Farmers Union, for each loaf of bread (average price $1.39), the farmer got *a nickel.* American farmers and ranchers receive only nineteen cents of every dollar spent on food. That's down from thirty-one cents in 1980.

None of this is on the radar screen of the American grocery shopper, who's perfectly happy to enjoy the lower prices and think no more about it.

As good as things are for the American food consumer, there is a misguided resentment toward farmers and the farm subsidies that make a cheap, abundant food supply possible. I used to feel the same way, until I started going to farm auctions and watched grown men holding back the tears as their tractors and land were sold to pay off the bank.

These are tough people. Giving up is not in their nature. But when the auctioneer sells off land that has been in the family for a hundred years, these people feel like they've let entire generations down. It's the same story elsewhere in rural America. Bankruptcies, divorces, and suicides are up.

Like other Americans, I'd heard the stories of "superfarms" getting outrageous subsidies. Some of that was true, and it was bad for the family farmer who wasn't getting a fair shake. So get this: A Democrat—North Dakota Senator Byron Dorgan—and a Republican—Charles Grassley of Iowa—got together to cap subsidies at $275,000.

Another misconception that fancy-pants big-city editorial writers never bothered to research is that, while it's true that subsidies *do* go to a minority of farms, that's strictly because of the USDA definition of a farm. Under the current regulations, to be considered a farm, all you have to do is sell $1,000 worth of agricultural products a year. That's basically a big vegetable garden! Sixty-three percent of the outfits collecting these subsidies are essentially hobby farms. According to Senator Kent Conrad (D-ND), of the 2.1 million farms USDA lists, only 16 percent—350,000 farms—have sales over $100,000. That 16 percent delivers 80 percent of the U.S. agricultural production. Sometimes, even when they mean well, journalists can create myths that are almost impossible to kill. The American farmer is the victim of such mythmaking.

Only about 30 percent of U.S. Department of Agriculture spending goes toward farm programs. Let's put that into perspective. The average American taxpayer pays about $23.50 a day to support the federal government's endeavors—defense, education, social programs, bail money for Bush cronies, and so on, bike repair, having the horns on Dick Cheney's head filed down . . . the usual.

Total federal dollars spent on subsidies in the 2002 Farm Bill account for 0.56 percent of the federal budget. Forty-four percent of the of USDA's expenditures fund things like school lunches, food stamps, and other programs that have a positive impact on one out of six Americans, many of them children. That Farm Bill feeds you!

You won't hear that story anywhere else. When a caller snuck by Limbaugh's screener one day and asked about the Farm Program, Limbaugh hemmed and hawed like a teenager on his first date. You could almost see the bedlam in the producer's booth as they scrambled to download something—*anything*—as Rush sputtered the party line about evil subsidies. Farm policy isn't a bullet point, but it ought to be.

The American farmer doesn't *want* to be subsidized. He can compete. Our farmers can work longer and smarter than anyone. But in a global market, he is burdened by unfair trade agreements. Our negotiators have used agriculture as a sacrificial lamb for years. They have traded away the farmer and the small towns he supports. Our negotiators haven't just traded away manufacturing jobs in the city.

They've traded away the heartland.

These are more than sad stories in desolate places. These sad stories hold implications for you and your family. Today, oil companies and OPEC have stripped middle America and the poor of some of their freedoms. In this case, it's a financial limitation that's crippling the caretakers of America's breadbasket. What kind of world will your children grow up in when a powerful few control the food supply? In the heartland, we'll cope. We can live off the land. The most vulnerable Americans, ironically, are those in urban areas—the most uninformed about food policy in this country.

What happens when a family loses its farm? Somebody buys it. Farms get bigger, machinery gets more powerful, and less manpower is required to work the land. That, too, drives nails into the coffins of small towns. If you look at a map of outmigration in America, you will see the center of the country emptying, from North Dakota to Texas. As farmers leave the land and manufacturing jobs are eliminated, small towns are dying. These small towns are the greatest places in the world to raise families, and we're losing that.

Senator Dorgan has introduced a new Homestead Act, modeled on the 1862 policy that offered settlers free land if they stayed and improved it for five years. Of course, today the land is all owned by *someone*. But Dorgan envisions helping families with tax credits and venture capital to buy homes and start businesses. We know we're not going to save every town in decline on the Great Plains. But after what these people have contributed to this country, it's not right to let them fade away without trying to help.

Some of the attrition is natural. The advent of big machines inevitably cut back the number of people required to farm a given plot of land. But much of the decline is because of economic selfishness on the part of big businesses that can't see past the bottom line. We need to stop the relentless consolidation of family farms, by assuring that a farm need not be a giant to compete.

Technology revolutionizes every industry. No one is going to stop it. No one *wants* to stop it. But we need to understand the implications of what's happening on the land. It's putting us in a precarious position.

Corporate farms that contract with food giants like Cargill can control the food from the field to the grocery store. Check the labels on your food packages. You'll be surprised at how often the same names pop up.

This kind of consolidation has already transformed the pork and poultry industries. Now, the major meat packers are trying to capture the beef supply as well. According to the USDA, four packers—IBP, ConAgra, Smithfield, and Cargill—handle 80 percent of all steer and heifer slaughter. Because no administration has tried to break up these monopolies, ranchers have had to fight back alone. And God bless them, they won one in 2004 when, in *Pickett v. IBP*, an Alabama jury awarded $1.28 billion to cattlemen in a class action suit because IBP had used captive supplies to negatively manipulate cattle prices. (Unfortunately, a judge reversed the decision.)

Tyson, the poultry monopoly, acquired IBP in 2001, further concentrating their control of the meat industry. According to a Tyson press release before the merger, the Arkansas company was already "the world's largest fully integrated producer, processor and marketer of chicken . . . with 68,000 team members and 7,000 contract growers in 100 communities." According to that news release, IBP, Inc., with $16.9 billion in sales, was already "the world's largest supplier of premium fresh beef and pork products, with more than 60 production sites in North America, joint venture operations in China, Ireland and Russia and sales offices throughout the world."

R-CALF USA, a cattleman's organization, led the charge in the lawsuit. Said Sam Britt, a Pasamonte, New Mexico, rancher who testified in the trial, Tyson/IBP "took over the chickens and hogs, but they found out cowboys weren't going to roll over and play dead for 'em!"

Herman Schumacher, a livestock market owner in Herreid, South Dakota, and the director of R-CALF, noted in ominous detail that despite packers buying artificially low, "consumers are being equally harmed as they have not realized any economic savings from the significantly lower prices packers are paying for cattle!"

Think about that. Has the price of your Angus rib eye gone down at the grocery store? In a truly competitive market, consumers would benefit. When these food conglomerates tighten the noose of market control around your neck, as has happened in the beef industry, they'll do to you what Enron did in California. Monopolies are inherently bad: Like any government with too much power, they will eventually use it. Corporations aren't bound by a constitution. They have one rule: Profit trumps everything.

Consumers had better hope that these cattlemen win their fight against these Goliaths. I'll say it again: *When these monopolies own the food supply, they'll own you.*

Where's the government in all of this? Squarely on the side of big business and foreign interests, as usual. Secretary of Agriculture Ann Venemen—I think of her as the secretary *against* agriculture—has not been a good friend to the American farmer. When one Mad Cow disease-infected dairy cow was discovered to have entered the United States from Canada, Venemen circumvented an embargo by allowing Canadian boxed beef into the country—which of course lowers the prices American cattle producers receive.

I have faith in our American producers and the safety of American-produced food, but testing each carcass makes sense. It would reassure consumers here and abroad. Some nations continue to close their borders to U.S. beef in the wake of that *one* infected cow in Washington State. So why does Venemen oppose even voluntary testing?

Maybe because that would put big-time packers at a disadvantage. The USDA says Mad Cow cannot be detected in cattle younger than thirty months, and most cattle slaughtered for human consumption are younger than that. Even if an animal was in the incubation stage for Mad Cow, the scientific community says it cannot be transmitted until much later when the cow shows the physical effects of the disease and starts wobbling like Paris Hilton at 2 A.M. So, at $30 per test, it's a waste of money, the USDA says.

If you believe the science, and I do, what's the harm in voluntary testing? Well, that would open the doors to smaller, specialized packers who want to sell to Japan, leaving the Gang of Four packers out in the cold. Unbelievable. The USDA is stifling the little guy, who has a better product and is willing to prove it. It's typical Washington behavior: Protect big business at all costs. Screw the little guy.

With the shadow of Mad Cow hanging over American beef, exports are down, even as our markets are flooded with beef from around the world. You, the American consumer, have *no idea* where the beef you are eating comes from. You know your jockey shorts come from China. But that New York strip? Anybody's guess.

One way to gain American consumer confidence is what's known as COOL—country of origin labeling. American-produced food is the safest in the world, but American producers are not rewarded by shoppers who want to buy American because country of origin labeling (which is the law, by the way) has not yet been implemented by the Bush administration. Why? Because their friends in the monopolized food industry don't want you to know where the hamburger you eat is coming from. Mexico? Canada? Australia? Argentina? They don't want you to know, because they ain't buyin' American!

The Food and Drug Administration damn near had a meltdown at the thought of Americans somehow getting "substandard" Canadian drugs (manufactured by American drug companies) at a discount. But burgers and ribs? That's another story.

Everybody gets protection except Joe Six Pack. Shut up and eat your hot dog.

Farmers and small businesses need a real chance to trade. Yet, government policies are inconsistent. We're willing to gut the middle class to enrich Wal-Mart through free trade with China, a country with a terrible human rights record, and yet the Bush administration drags its feet on trade with Cuba, a scant ninety miles off shore. Where's the logic in it?

I was the only American broadcaster to do a live show from Havana, when Minnesota and North Dakota flew trade delegations to Cuba in 2002. I don't know how many times that's happened since Castro seized control of the country. But I knew it was important for me to be on the ground to watch this initiative up close.

What was the purpose of the trip? The delegations were approaching Cuba on behalf of American farmers, who wanted to secure cash deals for sales to Cuba. Cubans needed the food. Our stubborn embargo policy has deprived the Cuban people of food and medicine. American farmers need the business. Some estimates said trade between Cuba and Minnesota and North Dakota could bring $80 million to farmers in those states.

For struggling farmers, a Godsend. Everybody wins, right?

Nope. Powerful anti-Castro sentiment in Florida continues to throw up roadblocks to any meaningful trade with Cuba. Bush knows he needs Florida to win—as history has shown. He's not eager to rock the boat. So, once again, partisan politics take precedence over what's good for the country.

With the 2004 election drawing closer, Bush further tightened travel restrictions to Cuba, allowing Cuban-Americans to visit relatives only every three years, and dramatically restricting the amount of money they can spend in Cuba. Imagine being separated from your family for three years . . . It's cruel.

When Wendy and I flew to Cuba on a plane loaded with Cuban-Americans, it was the beginning of a profound experience. I'll never forget the joy in that plane when it landed. They cheered and sobbed with excitement. When we went through customs, the Cubans were pressed up against the fence looking for their loved ones, and when they spotted them, there were more tears and hugs.

The people in Havana were very kind and friendly. Havana itself was like stepping back in time: No McDonald's, no modern cars. It was an enchanting city. When I hear news about Cuba, I don't think about Communism or Castro. I think about those joyful reunions.

The way Bush plays politics with both the Cubans and their relatives in America is a travesty. Every president since Kennedy has maintained a bitter hard line against Castro. In 1962, of course, our

Cuba policy nearly ended in Armageddon. In *Hegemony or Survival,* Noam Chomsky discusses a 2002 conference in Havana attended by many involved in the Cuban Missile Crisis: "A guy named [Vasili] Arkhipov saved the world," said Thomas Blanton of the National Security Archive in Washington. Arkhipov, a Soviet submarine captain, blocked an order to fire nuclear-armed torpedoes on October 27, 1962, during the tense standoff. The world almost ended on October 27, 1962.

Even after enduring forty years of isolation, Castro has managed to provide free medical care and college education to his people. The time has come to open the doors of commerce to Cuba. Castro is no saint, but I'm not sure he deserves a seat at the Axis of Evil table, either.

We don't have to abandon our human rights principles. We can continue to work toward that end. But we had better be consistent in our efforts. Think of what we've done with China, for instance. We even have trade and tourism to Vietnam, for cripes' sake! Even John McCain was able to forgive and forget.

And if you really are worried about human suffering, Mr. President, visit the western Dakotas the next time you're out hustling votes. See how our people are faring. Tell them, to their face, to tough it out. This isn't about Communism anymore. It's about politics. It may be good for George W. Bush and his aspiring-president brother Jeb.

But it's no good for America, or the American farmer.

When the Farmer Can't Feed Himself, Something Is Wrong

I'll admit it. I'm a romantic about the Old West. Spending time in western North Dakota during hunting season gives me a chance to rub elbows with real cowboys—the kind that speak with a bit of a twang, walk bowlegged, wear cowboy hats, and chew tobacco. Except for the spitting part, they are a striking piece of the landscape.

As I've confessed earlier in the book, I didn't always have that appreciation for the American farmer and rancher. Remember, I used to be a *conservative* talk show host: My conversion to liberal thinking didn't happen in a flash of light. It came to me as a result of my experience, of opening my eyes to things I had not seen before. I once bought into the mind-set—which you can still see on opinion pages of eastern newspapers, written by people who wouldn't know a cow if it kicked 'em in the ass—that farmers are essentially welfare recipients. Nothing could be further from the truth. The real truth is, it's not the American farmer who is subsidized. It's *you,* the American consumer.

The men and women of the heartland are under assault by unfair trade agreements and price-fixing, monopolistic, multinational food conglomerates. Then, when Mother Nature turns on them, it becomes the type of disaster you don't hear about.

When the president was working so hard to defeat Tom Daschle's protégé, Senator Tim Johnson, in the 2002 South Dakota midterm election, Bush made so many visits he could have qualified for a resident hunting license. He was regularly pestered by the press and officials to address the murderous drought that had dried up the western Dakotas. It was far worse than any living person could remember—statistically, the region's worst in four hundred years. There was no rain to grow crops. Cattle had no grass to eat. In short, farmers and ranchers had no income to pay for the basic necessities, let alone the operating loan at the bank. Suicides, depression, spousal abuse, and divorce were up. Bankruptcies shut down land that had been in the family since the Homestead Act opened up the country during the Civil War.

And yet, when the president was asked for relief, he essentially told farmers to tough it out. Sacrifice, he said. When one looks at the wasteful spending under this administration, that's hard to swallow. Under this administration, GI Joe, the American farmer, and Joe Six Pack have been doing an awful lot of sacrificing—and not reaping a whole lot of reward.

Bush's unspoken message in 2002 was that as long as South Dakotans were represented by the Democrats, Bush wasn't going to do squat. On the other hand, with California wallowing in massive debt under Democratic governor Gray Davis—much of it caused by Bush crony Ken Lay's Enron sharks—the unspoken message was again clear: *Choose a Republican in the recall election, and maybe I'll throw you a life preserver.* Bush plays politics with innocent people's lives.

When I started hearing more and more about what was happening in the western Dakotas, I decided to broadcast a show from Hettinger, North Dakota, to get their story out. Florence Hoff, a Presbyterian minister from Lemmon, South Dakota, a community about thirty miles from Hettinger, told me how local food pantries had been emptied by proud farmers and ranchers doing what their president had told them to do—tough it out.

The night before I did the Hettinger broadcast, I met with a group of struggling ranchers. Florence, who runs a food pantry in Lemmon and another in Bison, South Dakota, got calls urging her to attend my meeting. She said later that she hadn't intended to attend. She serves two congregations, she runs the food pantries—she's busy. But she kept getting calls. "I finally decided God wanted me to go," she said. I know the Lord is supposed to work in mysterious ways, but who'd have thought he works through Big Eddie once in a while?

But something magical did happen. Florence went on my show the next day, talking about the heartbreak going unnoticed in America.

"What we have is working poor," Florence said. "Both parents work, but even then, they aren't making enough to make ends meet. Families come to the food pantry because with the kids home for summer vacation, that's one more meal they can't afford. Most families in the area qualify for reduced school meals—that's part of the Farm Bill that doesn't get talked about.

"I've had people cry when they get the food," she says. "It means so much." Because Florence and her husband live in their own home in Lemmon, fourteen years ago she asked the church council if she could turn the parsonage into a food pantry. Two years ago, when she discovered families were driving as far as one hundred miles to get to the food pantry in Lemmon, she decided to open another food pantry in Bison, about forty-five miles to the southwest. She *had* to move the food closer to the people. With gas prices so high, she says, "They couldn't afford to drive to get the food."

The last time I heard from Florence, she had opened the food pantry in Lemmon for two hours. Fifteen families showed up. In that sparsely populated region, her food pantries serve an average 120 families a month. These aren't lazy people. "It's just a real struggle emotionally when they don't know where the food is coming from—where the next meal is coming from," she told me.

That's what really ticks me off. These people *know* how to tough it out. They've been toughing it out for a lifetime. They fight blizzards to get to their cattle in calving season. They're up before the sun in the morning, and often they're still working when the moon is on the rise. These are self-reliant, proud people. If *they're* asking for help, you can damn well be sure there's a problem.

I talked to one rancher after the Hettinger broadcast, and I don't suppose I'll ever forget the look in his eyes. "Look at me," he said. "I've lost almost a hundred pounds. I've lost my wife, and now I think I'm going to lose the ranch." It was a typical story, from a group of people so decent and kind they would give you the shirt off their backs. Pastor Hoff said, "It's a sad day when the people who produce the food for the world have to come to the food pantry to be fed."

These people struggle with depression. Some sit every night contemplating suicide. And the pressure of it all breaks up families. "We don't know a lot of what goes on behind closed doors," Florence Hoff says.

It isn't just the Dakotas that have been hit hard. Virtually all of western America is suffering from drought. The drought means that with no grass, the ranchers have been forced to sell their herds. The irony is, cattle prices have gone through the roof. Now, these debt-ridden ranchers can't afford the cost of building another herd.

"Once the cows are gone, they're gone," says Ted Uecker Jr., a second generation cattle buyer from Hettinger. "It's pretty tough to replace a herd that's been bred for two or three generations." Still, Uecker counts his blessings. Bad as it is in his area, "By God, you ought to see what it's like in Wyoming and eastern Montana! It's drier than hell."

Uecker learned the business of buying cattle off the ranch from his father, who set up shop in Hettinger in the mid-1940s. Today, "Teddy Bill," as he's affectionately called, knows every ranch and rancher within hundreds of miles. He watched one old friend sell off the family herd in late June 2004. "Those cows have been in the family since the 1940s," he said. "That's how frickin' dry it's been. Two hundred and fifty cow-calf pairs gone. Boom. They're outta the cattle business." That herd might have been saved, Uecker said, if "the goddamn government" had opened up idled Conservation Reserve Program land for emergency hay earlier than August.

It's folks like these that Florence Hoff is seeing at the food pantries.

As a measure of these people's pride, Florence told me about tough ranchers, hat in hand, quietly asking at the food pantry—not for a handout—but to exchange some frozen beef, which they are able to butcher themselves, for powdered milk, cereal, maybe some tuna. It broke my heart to hear that.

The day after Florence appeared on my regional radio show, which hits seven states and three Canadian provinces, her mailbox was filled with checks from all over the region. "We're still operating on that money today!" she said.

I'm so proud that my radio program was the vehicle that opened people's hearts and wallets. "People *do* care," Florence said. "I really do believe that, given the opportunity to help, they'll help. I truly believe that."

When I got back to Fargo, we organized a food drive. Maybe in the grand scheme of things, one semi-load of food wasn't going to make a big dent, but it sent a message that someone—a whole lot of people—cared. Farmers who had extra hay sent it to the dry areas, allowing ranchers to hold on to some of their herd.

But you know what? The thing got bigger than I could ever have imagined. After the program, semi-load after semi-load of food started arriving at Florence Hoff's door. A chicken processor from Minnesota contributed chickens. A potato farmer out of Fargo sent a truckload of potatoes. John Morrell, the meat processor out of Minnesota, sent a load of food. It got so big that Florence eventually had to call Lemmon Livestock, an auction yard where cattle are sold by farmers to cattle buyers, and ask to use their facilities to unload the semis. A bunch of volunteers gathered to unload as many as three semi-loads at a time. It was like an assembly line of hope. The food was packed into pickups and sent out into different neighborhoods.

But there was one challenge: How do you get people down on their luck to accept the needed food?

That Florence is a sly one. To start, she said, "We gave a box to everyone in the neighborhood. That made it okay." Some of the needy aren't even ranchers. They're the elderly, living on Social Security. "A very common amount they live on is $500 a month," Florence said. "I saw one as low as $199 a month. These people often have to choose between medicine and food on the table." Now, with luck, they're getting both more often.

The seed for all of this wasn't me. It was Florence. All I did was shine a little light on the crisis. People stepped in and did the rest.

Finally, after three years of drought, it rained three inches within a few weeks in July 2004. Ted Uecker says, "That rain saved us!

And you know how it is. The good operators—the ones with a few bucks set aside—they'll pull through. These old Norwegians are lucky. They always seem to get just enough rain to scrape by. They'll be cutting crops for feed, though. There won't be anything for the bin."

But sometimes even the good operators get hit so hard they can't recover. Uecker, who has seen more than one drought cycle, tells of watching old men and women selling off their herds in the early 1970s, holding back their best cows, hoping until the bitter end for some sort of divine intervention. When the last of the cows were sold, Uecker remembers the tears in the eyes of the old couples at the auction barn.

"This ain't the driest it's been," he says—because he's an optimist. But when you've sold your herd and you're out of the game forever, that doesn't mean much.

"So many people are leaving the area because they just can't make a living here anymore," Florence Hoff told me. She has continued to work tirelessly. She enlisted me to help out with a turkey program for the holidays. She also connected with a great outfit called Family-to-Family (www.family-to-family.org), a nonprofit hunger relief program for "profoundly poor and hungry families in the United States." The program matches sponsoring families with needy families. FedEx ships the food free.

Florence is especially enthusiastic about the fact that the poor and more affluent families involved communicate. That human connection means as much as the food, clothing, books, and medicine. "I think some of them are more excited about the letters than the packages," Florence said. Those letters are food for the soul. The first group of families to help the Western Dakotas was from San Diego.

Family-to-Family was started by Pam Koner from Hastings-on-Hudson, New York. In 2002, she saw a story in a newspaper about a poor community—Pembroke, Illinois, where people were starving. That's right—starving, in America.

The *CBS Early Show* interviewed her after she started the program. Pam told her family, "I've just read something that has moved me to tears, and we have to do something." She explained what she did: "I have a child-care program and about a hundred and fifty families that I'm connected with, so I came up with an idea: Why don't each of us commit to sponsoring a family in Pembroke, one-to-one, and sending one box of food each month to meet that need?" So Family-to-Family was born. A news story touched Pam Koner, and she has touched the lives of my friends in the Western Dakotas.

Who says there's no hope for America? People like Florence Hoff and Pam Koner give me hope. I believe in the American people. I believe in you! We can fix this thing. I know it.

Not long after my visit to Lemmon and Hettinger, Florence Hoff sent me a homemade plaque that said some nice things about me. A stalk of wheat was glued to the document. Now, I've got some impressive plaques on the walls of my office. I was named Broadcaster of the Year in 2000 by North Dakota Farm Bureau, and in 2001 by the North Dakota Grain Growers Association for my support of farmers. The radio station has a trophy case of such things. But that plaque from the people of the western Dakotas means more than most. It means I made a difference.

You see, *experiences* changed my outlook. And though I have argued that I don't see mainstream media as overtly liberal, something a journalist friend of mine said to me made sense. He said, "The real question is not whether the mainstream media is liberal—the question is, if they are, why is that so?"

It's not because there's any liberal litmus test to become a journalist. Righties fill out applications just like Lefties. But consider the life of a journalist. He is educated on more topics than most citizens—and, I'll bet, most elected officials. A journalist has to know enough about a topic to explain it to his audience. If he gets it wrong, people will know. So these people see the inner workings of government. They see the problems, they witness the disasters, and pretty soon their experiences tell them things need to change. A liberal is a compassionate proponent of change. So if journalists are liberals, maybe it's reasonable to assume it was their life experiences that changed them.

That's how it worked for me.

FEEDING THE NATION SOLUTIONS

• *Food conglomerates:* Bottom line, we need anti-trust legislation. The wide-open world of business has led to a company-gobbling-company frenzy that won't stop until we do something about it. This problem is pervasive in almost every industry. In the food industry, even more than in health care, the Third Pillar is a matter of life and death. We broke up the phone company. We need to do the same here. Or, at the very least, we need to make sure that these corporations are tightly reined in. I'll say it again, I don't think that big is always bad when it comes to business. It *is* hard to say when exactly a company has crossed the line from competition to predation.

   More often than not, however, the bigger the firm, the more little people are getting hurt.

• *Food policy:* The best thing we can do to ensure a fairer market is to ensure the survival of the American farmer through disaster relief when it's needed. Of course, there are things *you* can do to help out on a more personal level—such as sending a check to the food pantry, care of Florence Hoff, 11 Third Avenue West, Lemmon, SD 57638. Or contacting Family-to-Family via their web site (www.family-to-family.com).

The biggie is fair trade. Our farmer needs to have the same markets open to him that are open to the United States. It's not fair to allow virtually unlimited foodstuffs from markets not open to American products. I believe that the American farmer would prefer, eventually, to operate without subsidies. But when a European country subsidizes his farmer to the teeth, it has the same effect as outsourcing jobs. It takes away jobs at home.

- *Organization:* Freedom is great. We all want it. But we also need organization. There's a difference between freedom and inde- pendence when it comes to the American farmer. His sense of in- dependence has made him vulnerable. He sold his grain when he damn well wanted to. He sold his cattle when he wanted to. But eventually, especially after the economic farm crisis of the 1980s, farmers sold at harvest because they *had* to. The bank loan had to be paid. The big failure of the American farmer is that he did not organize well enough to gain the marketing strength when he had the chance. Organizations like Farmers Union have done a fine job of lobbying for a fair Farm Bill, but they don't have the mus- cle—that is, the cash—to create a formidable marketing co-op. The farmer has to live on something while holding commodities to sell until the price is fair.

When dairy producers organized and cut production, it brought the price of milk up. I have a dream that someday soon an organization will be created that's strong enough to help farm- ers get a fair price. Maybe state agricultural departments could form cooperatives and fund the venture until it could stand on its feet. This would not rival a mega-corporation in scope, but it could make them play fair. That means the farmer gets a decent price. I want to put those food pantries out of business! I know what you're saying—"Hey, you mean all of this means I have to pay more?" In the short term, yes. But over the long term, you can trust the American farmer to be fair. Eventually, if these mega-corporations grow unchecked, the price you pay will be very high indeed.

More farmers are looking at niche areas—organic food and specialty crops. It's working for some. I hope so. If we lose the great American farmer and rancher, we're not just losing an industry, we're losing the heartland itself, a place I believe to be the moral center of this country.

- *Starvation:* I'm not just talking globally, but in America. Get proactive. Get your church actively supporting food pantries and global relief. The difficulty in getting food to starving people is the fact that war and political unrest is often the cause of the crisis in the first place. One example is Sudan, where many are starving. The political infrastructure does not exist to distribute the food. America, on the other hand, has always been able to organize for wars and emergency action. Can't we get the food to where it needs to be if we set our minds to it? There are global outreach programs. The United Nations is a player. But if America is so motivated, much more could be done if we really set our minds to it. You want to change world opinion about us? Let's prove we aren't so greedy. Let's try to make a difference in a good way. Bill Gates deserves applause for doing just that in India in the fight against AIDS. He's setting a great example.

    Politically, economic sanctions should be a very last resort. It punishes the citizens of a country for the actions of their leaders.

These decisions take lives. Be accountable for the actions of your country.

A friend of mine said something recently that really struck me: "Our government is a mirror of *us*."

Ouch. I need to drop a few pounds. And I need a severe attitude adjustment. Nothing changes unless you want it to.

THE FOURTH PILLAR
EDUCATING AMERICA

THE PROBLEM

On the topic of formal education, we're seeing the effects of the Second Pillar—a sound economy—on the Fourth Pillar. Middle-income families are struggling to send their children to college. We're not paying teachers enough, so our public school students are at a disadvantage—especially in poorer rural and urban schools. George Bush is underfunding his program, *No Child Left Behind.* But the big problem is that Americans aren't paying attention. Oh, I know you catch the news. But have you really sorted through it? Americans are not fulfilling the basic requirement of being a citizen. You have to know what your government and society is doing and understand it. That's a real education.

HOW DOES THIS AFFECT ME?

Well, we're back to the same old story. If you're rich, even if you're not that bright, you can still go to Yale. If you can't afford college, your paycheck won't ever be as big as it could be. Lexington, Kentucky, *Herald Leader* columnist Diane Stafford writes: "From 1979 to 2003, the inflation-adjusted hourly wages earned by high school graduates one to five years after they left school fell by 17.4 percent among men and 4.9 percent among women, according to an analysis by the Economic Policy Institute . . . Also, the report said, employer-provided health insurance for recent high school graduates fell from 63.3 percent receiving coverage in 1979 to 34.7 percent in 2002. Pension coverage fell over the same period from 36 percent in 1979 to 20.1 percent in 2002." That sort of downward economic spiral further weakens the working class, and the Second Pillar of a sound economy. When the federal government fails to fund your school, your local taxes rise. It's a blow to your wallet and to your child's education.

Nuts and Bolts
of Education

Remember how George W. Bush was going to restore honesty and decency to an Oval Office tainted by Bill Clinton's infidelities? The theory was that we need a president to lead by example. Hey, I go along with that. Our most revered presidents are remembered for their honesty.

Now, four years later, we've all got ample experience to draw upon in judging the integrity of the Bush White House.

What concerns me is that the man who wants to be known as "the education president" has so little apparent intellectual curiosity. This is a man who's confused by the respective roles of the executive, legislative, and judicial branches of government. Here's what George W. Bush had to say about it: "The legislature's job is to write law. It's the executive branch's job to *interpret* law." (The judicial branch, presumably, is the duck-hunting branch of the government.)

When it comes to setting an example for America's students, Bush says, "I glance at the headlines just to get a flavor for what's moving. I rarely read the stories and get briefed by people who probably read the news themselves." Excuse me if I take little comfort in the fact George W. Bush wants to take the lead in America's educational system.

Even when he's leading, I'm not sure what he's trying to tell me. As noted in the book *Bushisms,* edited by Jacob Weisberg, Bush has declared: "We want to develop defenses that are capable of defending ourselves and defenses capable of defending others." He has charged: "The illiteracy level of our children are appalling."

He makes me dizzy.

Bush sought the support of Senator Ted Kennedy in passing the *No Child Left Behind* act of 2001, which has the high goals of raising standards. Bush, however, has failed to fund the program fully (falling short by $9.4 billion), thereby placing more of the financial burden on states and local school districts. On one hand, Bush crows about the income tax cuts; on the other, he fails to note that taxes have gone up elsewhere.

What's it all about? *No Child Left Behind* has expanded the federal role in education. It sets performance benchmarks for students and teachers. It holds states and schools more accountable for student progress. One goal is to make sure that every student can read after the third grade.

The plan is gradual in its implementation. States must bring students up to a proficient level in basic subjects by 2013–2014, based on testing. If that fails to happen for two years in a row, students will be allowed to enroll in other public schools. Students in a school failing to meet standards in three consecutive years must be offered expanded educational services such as tutoring. Failure beyond that point could lead to outside corrective measures and, presumably, the loss of some autonomy by the local board of education to the federal government.

The bill also demands that teachers be "highly qualified" in each subject they teach by 2005–2006. For rural and urban schools, who often scramble right up to the first day of school to contract teachers, that's a concern. *Every* school tries to get the best teachers available. The fact is, some areas of the country and some school districts are less attractive. School districts in rural areas rely on some excellent teachers, who may not be qualified on paper in every subject but who serve their communities beautifully.

The goals of *No Child Left Behind* are noble indeed. But many school administrators point out that the program is a huge unfunded mandate. A study by Augenblick and Meyers, Inc. concluded that Indiana schools would have to spend 31 percent more per student—from $5,468 to $7,142—to meet the new "commendable" standards. In Maryland, the state was forced to boost spending by $1.3 billion to cover the 34 percent to 49 percent increase in the cost of educating students. A Montana study concluded that base costs would increase by 34 percent to 80 percent.

With so many states running in the red already, *No Child Left Behind* is a budget breaker—especially when the president falls $9.4 billion short in federal funding for the program. So don't start counting up your tax break just yet. Your state and local taxes will invariably rise to fund this mandate.

Philosophically, I wonder what happened to the conservative mantra of states' rights. Haven't large federal mandates always been anathema to the GOP? Not only does this program strip states and school districts of a measure of control, it demands a higher tax burden of its patrons. That, of course, is in keeping with conservative philosophies. They want to continue to reward schools that have advantages and penalize those already at a disadvantage.

William J. Mathis, superintendent of Rutland Northeast Supervising Union in Braden, Vermont, says in a Phi Delta Kappa study that *No Child Left Behind* hurts those school districts that need help the most—those in economically depressed regions and those with minorities.

> Students with large and diverse populations will find it most diffi-
> cult to show progress while schools with a breakout group in special
> education will find it impossible. Black students showed a 94 per-
> cent failure rate, while Hispanics registered a 68 percent failure rate.
> Students who received free and reduced-price lunches showed a 56
> percent failure rate. Schools labeled as "failing" will not receive their
> label because they have failed. Rather, schools will be branded be-
> cause they are in poor or diverse neighborhoods, because they are
> small and rural, because they are underfunded.
>
> Statewide achievement tests do not measure the vast expanse of
> curriculum set forth by states and school districts. Tests tend to
> measure those things that are *easy to measure,* in an efficient and
> economical way. *This means that the focus is on lower-order thinking
> skills,* with a light smattering of higher-order skills, such as writing a
> short essay. Schools and teachers, faced with ever-increasing de-
> mands to avoid the "failing school" label, will logically focus on the
> curriculum content that is most likely to improve test scores. Leav-
> ing aside the fact that these tests provide little useful instructional
> feedback, the inevitable results will be that the nation's curriculum
> will be narrowed and the level of expectations will be lowered.

Mathis concludes that schools desperate to meet *NCLB* standards will encourage their poor students to drop out. President Bush
himself has touted dramatic results of the principles of *No Child
Left Behind* in Texas. Upon closer examination, however, it's a very
different story. As CBS's *60 Minutes II* exposed, in Houston alone
the school system's reported 1.5 percent dropout rate was really

25 percent to 50 percent. A high dropout rate means higher crime and poorly paid uneducated workers, who will drain the economy in the long run.

While the National Education Association (NEA) and many school boards and administrators view *NCLB* as an unfunded mandate, NEA attorney Robert Chanin asserts in a February 2004 *American School Board Journal* article that the *NCLB* act itself says the federal government cannot "mandate, direct or control" a state or school district "to spend any funds or incur any costs not paid for under this act." He's urging states to join an NEA lawsuit on the grounds that that rule is being broken.

Mark Schaunaman, former president of the North Dakota School Boards Association, says that *NCLB* is, indeed, an unfunded mandate. It puts rural school districts, which are already facing precipitous enrollment declines, in the hurt bag, because it forces them to compete with larger school districts for qualified educators. In a rural district, a math teacher might have a minor degree in physical education and be asked to fill both positions. A larger school district can focus the teacher in a specific area much more easily. Before *NCLB*, a rural district might provide just the right niche for a teacher with a minor degree. "I think this is basically going to become a national competition for teachers," Schaunaman said. "Those with more money, and amenities, will have a greater advantage."

In effect, poor school districts are being punished for being poor.

One school board member, Reverend Louden-Hans W. Flisk of Sykeston, North Dakota, has fought to keep the school doors open in his small community of 300. The school board member has put his money where his mouth is. The Catholic pastor has given bonuses to teachers, and, according to the Fargo newspaper the *Forum,* wrote a personal check to recruit a science teacher, a position difficult to fill.

In the 2003 school year, he gave every teacher—ten of them—$100 bills each month school was in session. Flisk knows that when a school closes, a community dies.

Mark Schaunaman knows how hard it is to come by science teachers. A few years back, he and a school administrator searched the entire North Dakota University system, which includes eleven institutions of higher learning, and came up with "zero potential high school science teachers." None. In the entire state of North Dakota, which has a stellar college system, Schaunaman and the administrator could find only *two prospective* math teachers.

Schaunaman says he thinks university counselors must do a better job of advising young teachers about where the opportunities are. He says when his rural school of Ashley, North Dakota, has an elementary position open, "We might get forty applications. But a secondary opening might not produce one."

In the long run, as poorer school districts struggle to pay teachers more—and they want to if they can afford it—school boards may be forced to cut back on elective offerings like language, and higher math and science offerings.

No Child Left Behind can work with an overhaul. But it has to be fairly funded!

Another concern I have is over the apparent growing acceptance of privatization and commercialization of education. There are private companies that administrate and take over teaching functions for *entire school districts.* Maybe it's just me, but I don't feel good about our children being taught by the lowest bidder. The NEA warns we could reach a point someday when privatization would reduce the role of elected school boards to "glorified contract administrators."

I support NEA in its opposition to vouchers for private schools. Shifting dollars from public education to private not only diminishes public education, it circumvents the line between church and state by giving federal funds to faith-based schools. If you want to send Johnny to a private school, that's fine. But don't expect me to chip in to the detriment of the public school my child attends.

Of course, this is all just good Republican politics. It keeps the fundamentalist Christian wing of the Republican Party happy. I just wonder if they'll line up to support vouchers for Islamic schools any-time soon.

It seems to me that conservatives want to encourage segregation between rich and poor, Christian and secular. I believe there has been enough separation. Enough stratification. Public education has been the great mixing bowl of America. Integration worked. I know. I was part of it.

When I was a high school freshman, in 1969, I was bussed to Maury High School in Norfolk, Virginia. There were 1,800 students—65 percent of them black.

There was a lot happening in 1969. Vietnam was raging. Martin Luther King had been killed. So had Bobby Kennedy. I was primed—*preconditioned*—to expect that my experience in this school, which was in the heart of the slums, would be miserable. The rap was the black kids were intimidating. They wanted to fight. They ran in gangs.

As it turned out, none of that was true. I never saw any of that in four years. That opened my eyes in a big way. It opened my mind. And I think it opened my heart.

I had it pretty good in my life. Dad was an aeronautical engineer for Uncle Sam. He worked on the F-4 Fighter, and got a Presidential Citation for it. Mom taught English. I had four siblings, all older. We were white-bread America. And every day, I got to see the other side of town. I got to see another side of life.

I remember that smoking pot was big in those days. I never tried it. Really—I never even got as close as Bill Clinton. Hell, I was always afraid I'd *like* it. I'm a balls-to-the-wall type of guy.

Sports was the ticket for me. We had great sports teams. We learned to work together. We learned that a chain is only as strong as its weakest link. Becoming friends with so many other students, black and white, really broke down the barriers for me. I still feel today that I was blessed to spend four years of my life with those guys. When I go back to Norfolk, these are the guys I still hug, because they played such a big part in my life.

Over the years, as I looked back, I came to the conclusion that maybe a little social engineering was a good idea. It still astounds me that we have such racial divisions in this country. After what I experienced, I just can't believe that after three decades, we haven't come farther.

Public school plays a part beyond classroom education. It provides *life* education. That's why I'd like to see us get back on track with public schooling. Before we go any further, I want to let you know that I'm generally a fiscal conservative—at least when compared to today's Republican Party. I don't think just throwing money at a problem works. You have to have a plan. You have to spend wisely.

One place we need to open the pocketbook is for teacher salaries. In the next ten years, the public educational system will need *two million new teachers*. Will we find them—and will we get them where they're really needed? That's the hard part. Average teacher pay in America is around $43,000—respectable, but when you measure that pay scale with other professions requiring a similar level of education, teachers get the short shrift. The highest average pay is in California—about $54,000. Unfortunately, not everyone can teach in California.

In my state of North Dakota, where teacher pay is near the bottom, you'll find many first-year teachers starting at less than $19,000. Rural and urban schools struggle mightily with teacher turnover.

Salary plays a large part in teacher decisions to leave. These schools become the minor leagues for teachers. While there's something to be said for the enthusiasm of first-year teachers, experience is important, too. According to NEA, rural schools serve more than 40 percent of our nation's students, but receive only 22 percent of federal funding. (The same sort of inequity is experienced by rural hospitals when it comes to federal support.)

If public education is not in crisis on a national level, it's certainly approaching that point in many regions across the country. I agree with Bush's philosophy of demanding better results. But you have to fund the programs. You have to pay teachers. You have to give rural and urban schools a fair share of the funding. Failing to fund these schools drains these communities of brain power, people, and economic vitality.

If you connect the dots, you can see the downward spiral in rural and poor urban regions. Wages stagnate. Taxes rise. Teachers run through a revolving door. Not only does K-12 education suffer, but parents and students in economically depressed regions have a hard time paying college tuition which is approaching an average of $8,000 a year (including private and public institutions).

While our nation's economic policies and job outsourcing have stagnated middle-class worker paychecks, college spending is out of hand. Tuition in Massachusetts rose 24 percent in one year! Who do they think they are? Health insurance companies? Sixteen states increased tuition by more than 10 percent from 2002 to 2003. They keep going back to the well with tuition increases! It's outrageous and irresponsible. Because the cost of college has doubled in twenty years, according to a 2003 congressional study, *nearly half* of eligible college students in America cannot afford a four-year college!

Now that's a crisis. A two-year vocational college may be the answer for some, but as America continues to outsource blue-collar manufacturing jobs, the best opportunities will be in the white-collar sector. As more middle-class students are excluded from colleges the more affluent can afford, a permanent social stratification will take place. You want to know why wars are overwhelmingly fought by the poor and minorities? Because often the military is the best job available. But it's not right.

Take Bush, for instance. Without family political connections and financial backing, could he have attended Yale and become the leader of the free world? If that's not a cautionary tale against social stratification, I don't know what is. I'm not saying that there aren't plenty of smart, able, and decent rich guys. There are. But there are also plenty of rich dolts who surfed to the top on a wave of Daddy's cash.

We want the best and brightest at the highest rungs of business and government. By excluding so many via economic policies that are *of the rich, for the rich,* we do long-term harm to the country itself. If you take a hard look at what the rich guys running this country have done, they don't look that damn smart to me.

If we're going to be led by a rich man, let's make it a *smart* rich man, with his heart in the right place, with his head on his shoulders and not up his ass (to speak in a language Dick Cheney will understand). Yeah, I know John Kerry isn't exactly Mr. Excitement—and what the hell is going on, when suddenly Al Gore *is?!*—but Kerry's studious approach to issues is what this country needs to get off this detour to oblivion.

I've appreciated Kerry's approach to education. It is clear to me he understands what is at stake for America. He has proposed an annual College Opportunity Tax Credit of $4,000, which is about what it costs for an average *public* college or university. That levels the playing field for poor and middle-class Americans. It's a great idea.

Kerry's *Service for College* plan offers American students "the chance to earn the equivalent of their state's four year public college tuition in exchange for two years of service." Without getting shot at, even. AmeriCorps service would grow from seventy-five thousand to five hundred thousand under the plan. Duties would include helping educate students in troubled school districts, homeland defense and policing, national park service, and aid to senior citizens. Kerry says he'll pay for the $13 billion plan by making the student loan industry a bid process instead of one supported by federal subsidies and assured profit.

A bid process in Washington, D.C.? What'll they think of next?

One of the most attractive ways for the economically disenfranchised to get an education is still the U.S. military. Active duty members and veterans can get nearly $1,000 per month for education. The GI Bill for Reservists offers up to $276 per month for school.

Now, I applaud every benefit offered to our nation's soldiers. Our nation needs warriors. But I ask you, is it right that for some it is the only plausible way to get an education? Is it right that power and privilege can buy the right connections and help the elite dodge military service? Is it right that America's poor and minorities fight the battles in Iraq? Is it right that only one congressman's son, Staff Sergeant Brooks Johnson, eldest son of Senator Tim Johnson of South Dakota, is serving in Iraq? (Senator Johnson is the candidate Bush worked so hard to defeat in 2002.)

America must make higher education available to all, regardless of economic status.

Education Is an
Everyday Process

Up to now, I've pointed out many problems in our country, and
I've offered some commonsense solutions. Commonsense solutions aren't always easy, not always popular, and certainly
not always painless. It's like a trip to the dentist to fix a bad tooth.
You want to fix it *before* you get a toothache. (No, I'm not making a
case for preemptive strikes.)

So far I've covered three of the Four Pillars of a great nation—a
sound defense, economy, and secure food supply. The fourth, Educating America, is as crucial as the previous three, because if Americans are not educated about their immediate problems and those
looming on the horizon, they will be unable to fix them.

Some of the crises I've talked about are immediate, others less so.
But a good mechanic not only fixes the obvious problem, he does
regular maintenance and knows that a knock or ping can eventually
result in engine failure.

For me, education is an ongoing process. If I didn't learn something every day, I would be "worthless as tits on a boar," to use the

local vernacular. I was well-grounded in education. I wasn't the sharpest knife in the drawer—not in my class, not even in my family. But the importance of education was made clear to me by my mother, the English teacher.

Sometimes I am drawn to the inscription my mother wrote on the inside cover of a hardcover dictionary she gave to me for my 1972 high school graduation: "Presented to Edward A. Schultz by his mother in the earnest hope that he will develop a love for learning and appreciation for the resources available to him in the pursuit of knowledge and wisdom."

If the point of that message wasn't clear to me then, it is now. I hadn't finished yet—my education was just beginning! And while I think my mother was thinking of academics, I've come to understand over the years that experience is as good a teacher as my mother was—and she was a dandy.

In addressing this final pillar, I want to make a case that, as Americans, we must do a better job of educating ourselves. It ain't easier, it *isn't* easy. The dynamics of this information age continue to evolve. There's plenty of information out there. I just think we've developed information overload.

It was easier when I was growing up. We had the evening news and the newspaper and some radio news at the top of the hour. We had time to digest things. Nowadays, it's all too easy to get caught up in media frenzy. It feels like a new disaster is breaking every hour or so. I know this firsthand: I live, and work, in the bullet-point culture, too. My show is fast-paced. We paint in broad strokes. I provide solid information and opinions, but there's no time for nuance—even if the president did nuance. So is talk radio the best place for in-depth news? Nah. It's news delivered with equal helpings of entertainment, advocacy, and opinion, to help the medicine go down.

Not all media is created equal.

Rush Limbaugh and I play in an arena where we go out of bounds sometimes. You don't know where the edge is until you go over it. Traditional print journalism grew up with the mantra of objectivity and balance, getting both sides of the story and separating news from opinion.

You have to *consider the source.* If you're watching Sly Fox News, for example, you have to know that even though they're capable of presenting many stories objectively, and sometimes do, their obvious slant eventually emerges on almost every topic. Righties say the same about PBS and major TV news anchors. I don't see it, but I'm not saying it doesn't happen. But it's the rule with Fox News and the exception at the major networks.

My role is to let my listeners know what's happening. With luck, my analysis will help my listeners cut through the right-wing spin coming from the administration, which all too often goes unchallenged by reporters.

So, can you consider yourself educated on a given subject if your sole source of information is Big Ed? Gawd, no!

Unlike Limbaugh, though, I'll tell you that right up front.

Folks like Limbaugh and Hannity want to be your *only* source for information, because they know that if you do any serious investigation, you'll figure out pretty soon that they're full of shit. I find it hard to believe that Limbaugh himself believes everything he says. Here's what you have to do for yourself: Read the newspaper. Pick up a magazine you believe is fairly balanced. *Time* may seem overly conservative and *Newsweek* a little too liberal to qualify as 100 percent objective, but I trust that when it comes to tough stories, they will fall back on the basic journalistic rule of honesty and objectivity. I trust them to try, and if they try, they'll do fine.

Even the Internet is a place to get some education. But it's the Wild West out there. There are distortions, lies, and worse. Pick a reputable source. Looking at the Drudge Report won't kill you, or automatically doom you to a life as a butt-puckered conservative. It's so far to the right, any semi-objective human will see it for what it is. On the other hand, it's fun to visit mediamatters.org, which exposes in delicious detail every lie from the right on a daily basis. But I think they see a conspiracy under every rock, when I don't. That site is the brain child of David Brock, Democracy Radio adviser and frequent guest on the *Ed Schultz Show*. Brock's book, *The Republican Noise Machine,* is a solid exposé on the organized propaganda effort of the right. David says Chris Matthews and Tim Russert lean slightly to the right, and that CNN's Lou Dobbs leans *hard* to the right. Overall, I think they're pretty balanced. Sometimes even Bill O'Reilly can go long stretches without goose-stepping around the studio. However, watching Sean Hannity causes me to gnash my teeth and rend my clothing. (Isn't that Biblical? I threw that in for Sean.)

Go ahead. Flip around. Watch Sly Fox. Watch Lou Dobbs, who may be the only journalist in the country up to speed on the dangers of outsourcing America's jobs. Listen to Limbaugh before you listen to me. I can handle the scrutiny. I don't think he's up to it, though. Get your news from a variety of sources. It's part of the educational process. I believe that if people wake up and do that, there's hope for America.

The danger I see in today's culture is that, politically, people have dug their heels in so deeply that they don't want to open themselves to another side of any argument. *Newsweek*'s Robert J. Samuelson recently wrote a column that I found unsettling and accurate. Quoting a June 8, 2004 Pew survey, he said:

People are increasingly picking their media on the basis of partisanship. If you're Republican and conservative, you listen to talk radio and watch the Fox News Channel. If you're liberal and Democratic, you listen to National Public Radio and watch *NewsHour* with Jim Lehrer. . . . What's disturbing is that the news media may increasingly cater to their customers' partisan tastes.

Rightie or Leftie, I have a challenge for you. If you're really solid in your philosophy, what's it going to hurt to broaden your horizons and watch a variety of channels? Heck, I check in on Sly Fox News most nights, and aside from the uncontrollable twitch under my eye, it hasn't hurt me a bit.

The big thing we as a nation have to learn to handle is information overload. My mother had the ability all mothers have—that uncanny knack for filtering out superfluous chatter and childhood arguments around the house; otherwise we would have driven her batty! We all have these filters. You can break into a football fan's house, but if his favorite team is playing, he won't even notice until you steal the couch from under him.

I'm not saying we should tune out, but we need to fine tune our filters. We need to walk away from the one-eyed Cyclopsean monster once in a while. Read a book. Take a walk with your wife. Reestablish diplomatic relations with your teenager. (Ask him about the pink hair. That's always a good ice-breaker.) Bring some balance back to your life!

Look, nobody can tell you *exactly* how to find that balance—least of all a guy like me, whose life revolves around being informed. But what you can learn from me is not to just accept what you hear. Talk back to your television! Challenge what they say. Heck, I have conversations with Sean Hannity all the time:

HANNITY: Yada yada yada yada yada.

ME: Idiot.

HANNITY: *Blither blather blither blather!*

ME: Dumb ass.

Then I switch channels. Before there were remote controls, guys like Elvis just shot the television. While a hunter and supporter of the Second Amendment, I think that's a bit extreme and a real waste of televisions.

Media has changed dramatically over the past twenty years, and America still hasn't caught up. We've been swept up, but we haven't really allowed ourselves to step back and really catch a breath. Even in 1994, Ted Koppel said of the increasing din of electronic media voices, "We have reconstructed the Tower of Babel, and it is a television antenna. We now communicate with everyone and say absolutely nothing."

Of course, Koppel was there when it started, with ABC's expanded evening coverage of the Iranian hostage crisis—a program that became *Nightline.* Koppel became the permanent host early on, and a new era was born. Then, when Ted Turner took a giant leap with CNN, People laughed. "There's not enough news to go twenty-four hours," they said. They were right then, and they're right now. So CNN and the other cable networks filled the gap by creating opinion programs like *Crossfire*—which, in many people's minds, substituted for actual news. It was exciting. There was actual dissection of the news, something we hadn't really seen before. But it was *infotainment,* folks.

The news had seemed inscribed on stone tablets when delivered by Walter Cronkite. Now it was fluid. The line got blurred between news and opinion. It's still blurred, especially on Fox, where opinion is brazenly woven within the newscasts. If you do a Google search on the words *Neil Cavuto bias,* you'll find him reveling in his bias, in both the show transcripts and his online column. Explain to me how a Fox newsman can proudly proclaim his bias, between station promos that trumpet how fair and balanced Fox is? Operating on the premise that there's a liberal slant to mainstream media, Fox has taken a *just get even* approach to broadcasting. That's not fair and balanced. It's not journalism, either.

Why is mainstream media so consistently accused of a liberal bias? Because they report the news! In America today, just telling the truth is considered liberal bias. Bill O'Reilly nearly had a conniption over the *New York Times's* continuous front-page coverage of the Abu Ghraib prison scandal. *Liberal bias,* he said. Is repeatedly reporting the truth indication of bias? It's better than repeatedly telling lies.

What they say about idle hands being the devil's workshop applies to twenty-four-hour cable channels. With so much time to fill, as often as not they end up essentially *creating* news to fill it. And in the rush to get the story first—as we saw in the early days of the second Iraq War—they often get it wrong.

We have this blaring media monster that is often wrong. All the more reason for the news consumer to raise his level of sophistication. It's a necessity if this democracy is truly going to function. I understand why people have lost faith in media, but Fox News is not here to rescue you, as they intimate. They're a major part of the problem.

One source of the problem is that they've successfully created an Us vs. Them marketing theme—a little trick Limbaugh does masterfully, too. But if you accept their vision of the world of journalism—which lumps "the rest of the media" into one undifferentiated group—you're as guilty as they are. The picture is much broader than that. Americans have to do their homework. They have to examine their news source's credibility.

The *New York Times* and *USA Today* both have had recent black eyes with the discovery that reporters invented sources. Jayson Blair—a pox upon you! What Blair did played right into the hands of the righties, who point to mainstream journalism as both liberal and dishonest. But you have to give the *New York Times* credit for the public flagellation they gave themselves with their in-depth expose of Blair's sins. Now ask yourself this: When was the last time you heard Limbaugh, O'Reilly, Hannity, or anyone from Sly Fox retract or correct a statement? What? They're omnipotent? (Or is that impotent?) You've heard corrections from Dan Rather and all the other news anchors. Most large newspapers have a daily correction section—often on page two—to correct errors that appear in print.

But is that any surprise? Newspapers publish the equivalent of a novel every day! Of course, they make mistakes. According to the *New York Post,* Dick Gephardt is John Kerry's running mate. The order to run with the story reportedly came from Rupert Murdoch himself, who owns both the *Post* and Fox News. An isolated case of an owner with what he believes is a hot tip? Or a case of trained journalists taking direction from a trained billionaire? It's worth asking the question: In any big operation, there are tugging strings you don't see. That's why getting your information from a variety of sources and making your own judgments is crucial. (For the record, Murdoch also owns this book's publisher—which has published many political books, both liberal and conservative.)

Most editors want to correct mistakes. It's essential to their credibility. It also sends a message to the reader—the news is not always accurate. You have a better chance of getting it right if you get your news from a variety of sources.

Right-wing talk radio and Sly Fox are a backlash against a media that some people believed was too liberal and too big for its britches. I go back to Watergate and the *Washington Post's* Bob Woodward and Carl Bernstein. What they did was every bit as patriotic as any American has done. I see Michael Moore as a different kind of patriot, but a patriot nonetheless. For all the good Nixon did with international affairs—Lord, Bush could take some lessons from him—he put himself above the law. It was a major test for this democracy.

But it seems to me that the media got cocky after Watergate. There was less respect shown to the presidency, culminating with what happened to Clinton—a destruction of a presidency based on *personal* shortcomings. When you look back and see the barrage Clinton was under—some of it legitimate—how the hell do you make a case that the media was liberal? If they were, they sure didn't pull any punches on Clinton!

American Journalism Review quotes S. Robert Lichter, president of the Center for Media and Public Affairs, the independent group that did a study on Reagan, Clinton, and Bush II's presidencies: "*Bush is being treated normally for a president,* which is to say negatively. The media are tough on presidents."

I think when the mainstream American media slid into tabloidism, they lost more credibility with Americans, who, I think, have a sense of fair play. Even when people like Dan Rather resisted chasing sordid personal stories about Clinton, he was held up as an example of obvious liberal bias—because he didn't want to attack Clinton on what he thought should remain personal matters.

I believe our public officials do need privacy. We have raised the bar so high, though, that any candidate who has had a skeleton in his closet—and don't we all?—is so cruelly dissected by the press that he cannot survive the process. So we get second-raters who never made a mistake because they don't have it in them to try to do something bold. It is a ruinous process that keeps good people out of government and unfairly maligns many who run. I've been guilty of that, too. I've taken my cheap shots at Bush. Of course, his administration, under Herr Rove, specializes in cheap shots. None of this is good for the political process: It just muddies the waters for everyone.

I'd rather have a guy who has made his mistakes—and *learned from them.* That *learning* part is the key. If simply having made mistakes was the benchmark for greatness, Bush II would be a genius.

Some people say that JFK, with his mistresses, wouldn't have been able to survive in today's political climate. I disagree. He would have survived in much the same way that Reagan survived his very different personal shortcomings—on the strength of charisma. The cult of personality will always be the big swing vote. The media and the American people love to be charmed. With all the embarrassment Bill Clinton endured, he left office with the highest outgoing presidential approval rating ever—because he has charisma. That's what really infuriated the Righties. Nothing seemed to stick. (Limbaugh said Clinton had Teflon testicles—which I have to admit I do find funny.)

Humor aside, our country has become so polarized, so distrustful of politicians and the media who report on them, that it's led to real frustration—and, worse, apathy—on the part of the American citizen.

Three things have to happen to correct the course we're on. First, the politicians from both sides of the aisle have to be able to work together. I place most of the blame for the current atmosphere at the feet of George W. Bush, who has taken a "my way or the highway" approach to political discourse. A democracy (okay, technically, a republic) is about debate and compromise. It's slow, unwieldy, frustrating, and imperfect. But it *does* work. We need a populist president who can bridge the chasm separating our dysfunctional two-party system. Second, we need an alert, involved, savvy citizenry, willing to educate themselves on the issues. Third, the media must work harder to win back the trust of the American people. What good is the First Amendment right to freedom of speech if no one believes what you're saying?

A national council of journalists should be formed as a media watchdog. Annual reports about bias, accuracy, and dishonesty should be made public. Sure, I understand that judging bias is difficult. But *accuracy and dishonesty* are pretty clear-cut. I think Americans would be gratified to know how accurate the mainstream media are—and to have a record of how many times outlets like Sly Fox have gone off the rails. In effect, that's what www.mediamatters.org is trying to do—but they've got an agenda, too. An independent council of journalists would have to be comprised of a fair sampling from media sources. It would be like the creation of the Iraqi council: a monumental task.

It's a tough challenge—but a critical one, because the public is disenchanted. The University of Connecticut did a survey on the First Amendment in 2003 (excerpted in *Mother Jones*) in which 28 percent of Americans said that newspapers *should not be able to publish freely without government approval.* When that number reaches 51 percent, you can kiss democracy goodbye. Forty-six percent said that there's *too much press freedom.* The First Amendment goes too far, another 34 percent said. All of this pleases the neocons to no end. When the press isn't there to hold them accountable, they'll be able to do everything they want.

Big Brother is here.

But then, so is Big Eddie.

EDUCATING AMERICA SOLUTIONS

- *Public schools:* Accountability in education, which is the premise of the president's *No Child Left Behind* program, is a good idea, but an unfunded mandate isn't fair. By underfunding the program, local school districts and taxpayers have to make up the difference. We need to fund schools more fairly. Wealthy school districts can afford to offer more classes and other advantages. Schools in poorer districts are put at a disadvantage. Schools in the heartland often face a poverty-stricken tax base, low enrollment, and therefore less overall funding from the state and federal government. Plus, they run long bus routes to serve students. Overhead is higher; funding isn't high enough. The Department of Education has to take a lead role in providing equity. On a state level, we need to focus on equity, too.

- *Teacher pay:* Again, we need to look to the federal arm of education funding to help schools in tax-poor districts raise teacher salaries. States with the wherewithal can, and should, try to make a difference. One thing North Dakota did (*Do I really have to credit the governor with doing something?*) is to fund a $3,000 teacher salary increase. We're still near the bottom, but at least it was a step up the pay scale. These are key people in the fabric of America. They're the soldiers on the front line of education. We need to honor them and what they do.

    And one more thing: Every one of us should take responsibility for our child's education. Take away the kid's Gameboy once in a while. Kids don't read enough. Have him give you a weekly book report. He'll hate you now, but sing your praises later. (You know, I'm starting to sound all crotchety—just like I thought I never would back when I was part of the generation that scared the hell out of everyone.)

- *College:* Whether we adopt John Kerry's $4,000 tax credit plan—which I like because it helps the middle class—or if the Republicans come up with something better, it is absolutely imperative that every American who wants to go to college can afford to do so. As manufacturing jobs fly out of America, the best hope for any young American is a great education. The alternative appears to be a low-paying job in the service industry. Education means more brainpower for the country. More solutions. More ideas. A vibrant society. If Americans are denied education and training, the gap between the have-mores and the have-nots will eventually kill this democracy. Education is the great equalizer.

- *Cutting through the media clutter:* I've said we have media overload, and we do. But if you really become a student of the news and choose a balanced mix of sources, you're going to be better informed, and therefore a better citizen. And before you buy into the idea that the media is liberal or even my argument that Fox News is slanted, do something revolutionary. Go to the bookstore and look for a book by a journalism professor and find out how they're teaching journalism to their students. I think you'll be impressed. Then, when you look at the news, *you* can make an informed judgment about how liberal or right-leaning a source is. (And just think: When John Ashcroft gets around to reading your bookstore receipts, boy will he be impressed! Then again, if he thinks you're a journalist yourself, you might be bundled up in a canvas bag and never heard from again. . . .)

It all boils down to you. You have to separate the wheat from the chaff. Being informed isn't enough. You need to vote—and so does everyone in your neighborhood! Drive a bus to the polls! It doesn't matter which way they vote. If everyone votes, and we still go up in flames—well, then, at least *we* made the choice.

Conclusion

Revolution

Today, as I finish writing this book, it is July 4. I didn't plan it that way. It's just the way it worked out. I've said what's on my mind, and now I'll go back to concentrating full-time on my radio show. Somehow, when I signed on for this project, I never expected what I now find myself thinking: As I've sorted through America's problems, I didn't come across one that didn't have a solution. Sure, sacrifice is involved. But sacrifice has always been the price of freedom. In the end, the reward is greater than the sacrifice.

Today, as I write, there's a song I can't get out of my head—"Revolution" by the Beatles. "Weellll, you knooow," John Lennon sang, "we'd all love to see the plan." He was on to something: It's a lot easier to complain about politics than it is to come up with a better way of doing things. Some of the solutions I've offered here will take wiser men than me to sort out. I'm not waiting for some smart guy to ride in on a white horse and offer up a game plan. I know who's going to fix it. It's you. You and me and the rest of us who have been sitting back and watching the Four Pillars of a great nation erode.

Over my lifetime—half of which has been spent in America's heartland—now and then I would talk to an old-timer, someone who had lived through the Depression and the wars of the past fifty years. "If things keep headin' where we're goin,'" they would invariably say during the conversation, "there's gonna be a revolution."

I never understood where they were coming from. But I hadn't lived enough to understand. I'm like you. I could never imagine America being where she is today. But they could. I don't know if it was politics that made them think that. Or economics. But my gut tells me they were measuring the changes in each generation: The growing apathy. The indifference. The selfishness. It all grew and became acceptable. Greed has never been good. It's never been good for the soul. How can we go to church on Sunday, and then jump right back into the trading pit on Monday and start putting the screws to the system again?

After the American Revolution, Thomas Jefferson said, "God forbid we should ever be twenty years without such a rebellion." And he went on to warn about being uninformed. "If [the people] remain quiet under such misconceptions, it is lethargy, the forerunner of death to the public liberty . . ."

The last American revolution occurred during the 1960s. Americans rose up in protest against racial inequality and the war in Vietnam. It's been thirty years. We're overdue. I'm not talking about violence. I'm talking about social and political action.

In the beginning of this book, I devoted a great deal of time to the imbalance and outright lies of the right-wing media, in collusion with our neoconservative government. Why? Because it is so pervasive, so insidious, that the chances for honest action by honest people are being diminished daily.

Consider the source. The elitist frat boys of the current administration—and their corporate pals—don't think you're worthy of the truth. When a reporter asked the president what mistakes he thought he'd made, he couldn't come up with any. *What?* They should have called me instead. Man, ask this guy a tough question, and he acts like you pissed on his shoe.

I'm not demanding a confession, just an occasional reality check. But these guys will never admit a mistake. Maybe they're running for pope! You don't hear it from the administration.

You don't hear it from Sly Fox News. The other night I heard Sean Hannity tell the viewers that his network represents the way journalism ought to be.

I almost choked on my pretzel.

I hate to break it to you, Sean. What you're doing isn't journalism. Journalism isn't position statements disguised as questions in an interview. Real journalism produces substance. What Fox News has done is take right-wing talk radio and put it on television. It's a brilliant strategy. But it's not journalism. It's not balanced. And it's not ethical. Not if you're going to *pretend* it's journalism. Talk to Helen Thomas, Sam Donaldson, Tim Russert, or Mike Wallace. *They're* journalists. As the recent documentary *Outfoxed* showed, there are all too many former Fox employees out there who are willing to testify to Fox News's intentional and mandated conservative slant. It was no surprise. It's been obvious all along.

Right-wing talkers? They're actors delivering the party line in exchange for a paycheck. When Limbaugh delivered his speech at the National Association of Broadcasters convention in Philadelphia— and this was on the heels of the ESPN Donovan McNabb flap and his OxyContin mess—he had a great opportunity to tell them where the bear shits in the buckwheat. There, in front of all these shoot-from-the-hip talkers and on-your-feet thinkers, the icon of them all, Limbaugh, brought *a script.*

Don't *read* to me, Rush. This ain't Romper Room.

Man, when I get on stage, I don't need Peggy Noonan and I don't need crib notes. I *know* what's on my mind. And when I'm doing a radio show, I don't know who's calling and what they're going to say. I take them cold, because I revel in spontaneity. We screen calls for audio quality, but not for content. Call the show. We won't ask you what you want to talk about.

All those right-wing talkers out there know who's calling and what the topic is before they ever press the button. If they haven't done their reading on the subject, they don't take the call. That way the deck is stacked against the caller—just as the deck is stacked against middle America. And when a caller throws them a curveball, they sputter like my lawn mower on a cold morning.

These people will not admit that they don't know everything. It's disingenuous. It's showmanship. I don't mind being corrected on the air. You *disarm* the people who want to criticize you when you admit you don't know everything! Hey, I'm just a jockstrap who reads a little bit.

If you're reading this book standing up in a subway, sit down immediately! Plop into the lap of a stranger if you must. I'm about to do something never before done by a talk show host in America, and I don't want you fainting. It's unheard of. Shocking!

I am going to tell you I was wrong.

I supported the war in Iraq.

I made a mistake.

This willingness to reconsider a position has rocked the radio airwaves. Some people fainted. *The Ed Schultz Show* has created quite a buzz among the hardcore righties on the dial:

"What's his secret?"

"Something called honesty."

"That'll never work."

It would be funny if these people weren't so dangerous. A nation dominated by one political ideology is on a dangerous course. I don't want to muzzle the righties. This is America. But even activist talk radio needs ethics. Telling the truth would be a good start.

These people are not your friends. They do not consider you their equal. You are a rabble, to be managed and used. And they've done it successfully.

After 9/11, with the passage of the Patriot Act, our civil liberties are in peril. The neocons saw an opportunity, and they grabbed it. Congress literally passed the bill in the middle of the night; most of the members of Congress hadn't even read it! That's not how democracy works! I know the president doesn't read, but the whole Congress?

They let us down.

The Patriot Act, and the Patriot Act II, are waging a war on your civil liberties. The latter sought to overturn a federal court ruling that forced Bush to reveal the identities of those imprisoned since 9/11.

If Ashcroft had his way, secret arrests would be legal.

The Supreme Court slapped Ashcroft's hands on June 28, 2004, voting 8–1 that holding a citizen without due process of law isn't American. Justice Sandra Day O'Connor wrote: "It would indeed be ironic if, in the name of national defense, we would sanction the subversion of one of those liberties that makes the defense of the nation worthwhile." The high court also ruled 6–3 that prisoners detained at Guantanamo Bay, Cuba, must be afforded a hearing. That's good news. (The bad news is, Ashcroft still has "Attorney General" inscribed on his business card.)

The 2001 Patriot Act essentially dismisses the requirement of probable cause. The FBI can search and subpoena your personal records without you ever knowing it happened. Roving wiretaps may be placed on phones or computers that a suspect *might use.* In other words, Americans are suspects until proven otherwise.

Excuse me, but I checked, and the only Americans on the planes that hit the World Trade Center were *hostages.* Welcome to George W. Bush's America, where the people are the suspects.

This attack on the Bill of Rights is for your own good, they tell us. Just relinquish a little itty bit of freedom, and we'll take care of you. It's a deal with the devil. Benjamin Franklin said, "They that can give up essential liberty to purchase a little temporary safety, deserve neither liberty nor safety." Nobody is talking about any of this. Debate is not treason. I truly fear for my country if we do not swing back to the center.

America has faced threats to freedom and the Constitution before. Under John Adams in 1798, Congress passed the Alien and Sedition Acts. Fearing war with France (don't tell me you're surprised!). Adams suspected that spies had infiltrated the country. Thus began the hate portion of our centuries-old love-hate relationship with France. (Come on. These people gave us Brigitte Bardot. Doesn't that count for something?)

In 1942, Franklin Roosevelt ordered Japanese Americans into internment camps. He was wrong. Adams was wrong. And today, John Ashcroft is wrong.

After September 11, 2001, I understood for the first time how the German people could allow such atrocities to be committed in their name. *Why didn't they speak out?* They were in the clutches of fear. After the planes crashed into the Twin Towers and the Pentagon, a wave of uncertainty and fear swept this nation. The press was intimidated. They failed in their duty. A free press is all that stands between you and a dictatorship.

Limbaugh calls any parallel to pre–World War II Germany a "cliche." Rush, on the same program in which he invoked Abraham Lincoln's suspension of habeas corpus in the Civil War, said that Senator Edward Kennedy (D-MA) should be tried for *treason* for making that comparison. Okay, now I'm really confused. We can talk about the Civil War. But World War II is a cliche? Can I get a ruling on this? I know we can't bring up Vietnam, but I'm pretty sure we can talk about Somalia.

Ted Kennedy has been one of the clear voices articulating the truth about the Administration's slipshod handling of the war on terror. "Al Qaeda—not Iraq—is the most imminent threat to our national security," he said. "Our citizens are asked to protect themselves from al Qaeda with plastic sheeting and duct tape, while our Administration prepares to send forces to war against Iraq. Those priorities are wrong."

It was the old bait and switch. The Bush administration solemnly invoked 9/11 as they made the case for war in *Iraq*. As Kennedy noted, it was al Qaeda that attacked America. Attacking Iraq was like shouting "Remember the Alamo" and invading Canada.

As long as we're dusting off the pages of history, let's talk about Lincoln. People remember him for his honesty. During the Civil War, Lincoln *did* infringe on civil liberties; he broke the Constitution by suspending habeas corpus, which forbids illegal imprisonment without significant evidence of wrongdoing—just what the Patriot Act does. History has forgiven Lincoln because of his dire situation—and because he reinstated habeas corpus after the war.

The Constitution and the First Amendment were created by men who understood and had experienced tyranny. They knew that the greatest danger to a people was their own government.

The Constitution is not an *impediment* to liberty, as Ashcroft believes.

It is a shield from tyranny.

Among the nations of the world, America is moving into its teenage years. Adolescence is always a time of discontent, angst, apathy, and anger. (And pimples.) We all survived those years. Some were crippled by them. Democracy is a relatively new idea, and the aristocracy has never believed in it. They don't believe in it today. They don't think you're smart enough or well-informed enough to make good decisions. *They alone will rule!* So they use propaganda to stampede you.

The Bush administration and their pet talk show hosts pound, pound, pound the same message into the ears of the listener and viewer. It's not news. It's indoctrination. In the words of neocon poster child Joseph Goebbels, "The rank and file are usually much more primitive than we imagine. Propaganda must therefore always be essentially simple and repetitious."

This is nothing new. It's never reached this level in America, but history has valuable parallels. Germany brainwashed and cowed a desperate nation, which led to millions of deaths in World War II. Rome crumbled ultimately because of overextension and apathy. That's why I've paid so much attention to history in this book. We're living in historic times. Tumultuous times. Times change, but evil never does.

I know it seems overwhelming, but it's important for every citizen to grasp the importance of the Four Pillars—and to connect the dots between them. Defense is weakened by a bad economy. A bad economy weakens education. Undereducated Americans and their children endure the cycle of poverty. A corrupt economy threatens food supply. They're all intertwined. We cannot fix one without repairing them all.

But we can. America survived a Revolutionary War, even though there were times of hopelessness to follow. The Civil War was our greatest test. Then came World War II. Korea. *Vietnam.* And now this. We've prevailed—not in spite of democracy, but *because* of democracy.

Why do I have so much hope? It's because of the people I meet in the heartland and across the country when I travel. It balances my perspective. I, too, get swept up in the never-ending news cycle of tragedy and fear. Some days it all seems so dark, so hopeless. But when I get out and start mixing with real Americans and see their heart and goodness, I know there's hope for America. My callers give me hope. Every time I hear about someone doing something special—opening a food pantry, feeding the poor—it buoys my spirit.

I hear about first-class airline passengers giving up their seats to servicemen on leave, and I know this country still has the spirit to be great. I see Al Gore, cured of Dutch Elm disease, injecting life into the Democratic Party and asking the hard questions. A resurgent Democratic Party is good for everyone—not because a "liberal agenda" will dominate, but because debate and balance will be returned to politics. I believe most Americans are nearer to the center than the extreme left or right. And I think most of us understand instinctively that extremism in any school of thought is bad for the country.

Sure, we've hit a few rough patches in the past few years. And we're not out of the woods yet. But this country has a great heart. Regardless of the harm we've done in the world, I believe my country has done far more good than bad. I'm proud to be an American, and you should be, too. Heads up, chin out!

A sign of the times: The American Civil Liberties Union has sided with Rush Limbaugh, reminding us all that John Ashcroft ought to stay out of our personal records. America is coming together again. Holy smokes!

So where do we go from here? Well, you know your job: Be informed. Stay informed. Be vigilant. Get active politically. VOTE! And motivate others to do the same.

Start giving. Have a little faith. Even if money's a little tight this month, send a check to someone who really needs it. Do something for your community. Fix up a park, a playground. These things generate hope, and with hope we can do anything—*anything*.

It's easy. Just do one good thing a day. *One good thing.* It doesn't have to be big. It doesn't have to be monumental. Just do something selfless. If everyone—or even a small percentage of Americans—do that, we'll make it.

ED SCHULTZ
July 4, 2004

ACKNOWLEDGMENTS

No project as consuming as this book is successful without the vision and hard work of many people. First, and foremost, I am grateful to my wife Wendy, whose love and support has transformed my world. I wouldn't be who I am or where I am today without her.

I am honored to have a son as fine as David—a focused, determined, and respectful young man who inspires me. My wish for him is that he have a life as grand as mine has been with him in it. If there is one quality I hope I've passed on to Dave, it is that he always be a fierce competitor and never give up. The quality in him of which I am most proud is that he loves his God.

I am blessed, too, by five wonderful step-children, Megan, Christian, Joe, Greta, and Ingrid, who have become such a big part of my life in a very short time.

The national *Ed Schultz Show* could not exist without Tom Athans and Democracy Radio, who share a dream with me of bringing balance back to the airwaves. I owe a huge debt of gratitude to Amy Bolton, a vice president and general manager with the Jones Radio Networks, for having the insight to see that my voice could change the industry and the determination to make it happen.

Thanks to Paul Woodhull of Media Syndication Services, whose friendship and hard work helped me get through the very difficult days of the national show.

Along the path of my life, I have been blessed to have men like my Moorhead State University coach, Ross Fortier, to show me the way. In my radio career, previous KFGO owners Bruce Thome and Jim Ingstad and my longtime general manager, Dick Voight, have offered me leadership, friendship, and loyalty.

These days, I depend on three people to make *The Ed Schultz Show* run full tilt. First, my longtime board op, a real wizard, Tank McNamara, who leads the team in extradition warrants; second, James "Homey" Holm, my pale, Norwegian producer, who has a black belt in liberalism; and finally, my business manager, Jim "Bank Shot" Heilman, who has been watching my back for many years. Thanks, Jimbo.

Thanks, too, to publisher Judith Regan, editors Cal Morgan and Anna Bliss, and the rest of the exemplary staff at ReganBooks for helping my voice to be heard in a new arena.

I have a great deal of appreciation for my agent Al Lowman and his partner Bill Heinen for believing in me and my vision for a greater America.

Finally, I am grateful to my editorial director on this project, *Ashley* (ND) *Tribune* publisher and columnist Tony Bender, a good friend, devil's advocate, and huge pain in the ass, who challenged, pushed, and cajoled this sometimes tired and ornery talk show host to make my voice and philosophies sparkle on paper. *Now,* will you leave me alone, Tony? I've got some fishing to do.

INDEX